Asexuality: A Brief Introduction

From the pages of AsexualityArchive.com

Asexuality: A Brief Introduction

Version 1.0.120709

Contents

I am asexual.
I don't feel sexually attracted to anyone.
Not men. Not women.

That's all it is.

I'm not gay.
I'm not straight.
I'm not bi.

I'm none of the above.

Asexuality is real.
It's not fake.
It's not a hormone problem.
It's not a way of running from a bad relationship.
It's not a physical condition.
It's not an attention grab.
It's not an inability to have sex.
It's not an inability to love.
It's not some way to be "special".
I don't care if you have sex.
I don't care if you don't.
I don't want to shame you.
I don't want to convert you.
I don't want to recruit you.

I just want you to understand me.

I was probably in high school when I first realized that I was different.

It was a sunny day in the springtime. We were just coming out of the last chills of winter, but we hadn't yet started into the oppressive heat of the Nevada summer. On a day like this, many of the girls in the school would decide to begin working on their tans on the lawn in front of the school.

On this particular day, I was with a friend who decided he wanted to "check the weather" on the way to our typical lunch gathering point outside our next class. "Checking the weather" meant taking a path across the front lawn, even though that route was probably three times as long as the most direct path.

As we passed a concrete sculpture in the middle of the lawn, one of the girls lying on it called out a "hello" to me. She was in one of my classes, but I barely knew her. I nodded politely and kept walking. When we entered the hall on the far side of the lawn, my friend stopped me.

"Oh, wow, the weather was so hot today! You *KNOW* her?"

"Yeah, she's in my PE class."

"She's so hot! Why didn't you stop and talk more?"

"What about? Badminton?"

"Does it matter? *Didn't you see what she was wearing?*"

At that moment, the whole situation seemed odd to me. I knew that the purpose of the walk was to ogle the sunbathing girls, but it wasn't until right then that I realized that I had no interest in actually ogling the sunbathing girls. Moments earlier, I had looked right at a hot, well-endowed blonde, in a tight white shirt and black shorts that ended at mid-thigh, and didn't really pay any attention to her. That is not the reaction of a typical 15 year old boy.

I didn't think much of it at the time. It didn't launch me into an identity crisis. It didn't leave me wondering if I was actually gay. However, it did make me aware that sex really was a thing and that other people were more interested in it than I was. I had always been on the outside of all of the locker room talk and rumors about who was doing what with whom. The other boys would talk about their dreams of making it with so and so, but I never felt the same. This event made me look those conversations in a different light.

The closest I came to having a girlfriend in high school was the geeky redheaded girl in my math class. She was smart, liked my writing, had a subversive sense of humor, and wanted to save the world when she grew up. I never bothered asking her out, because I could never think of anything we'd do together if she said yes. I was satisfied just sitting next to her for an hour a day and occasionally talking about homework. I never secretly fantasized about her, I never pictured her naked, I never even thought about kissing her. When I did think about what she'd be like in bed, I always imagined her in comfy flannel pajamas, sleeping soundly.

It wasn't until after college that I got a girlfriend. Everyone else thought she was a knockout stunner, but the strongest word I could use to describe her looks was "cute". She hated that. She'd get upset that I didn't call her "hot", but I couldn't call her "hot", because I didn't feel that she was. She'd send me half-naked pictures or wear skimpy clothing in an effort to get me going, but nothing ever worked.

It took great effort on her part to convince me to do pretty much anything sexual with her. It wasn't resistance or fear, I just wasn't all that interested in taking part. And when I finally did get to rounding the bases, I had no idea what I was doing. For much of the physical side of our relationship, I felt entirely out of place, like I'd shown up at a 5-star restaurant wearing a t-shirt and sandals. Curiosity drove me more than any particular urges. I wasn't particularly enthralled by seeing her naughty bits. Touching her breasts was about as exciting as touching her shoulder. I distinctly remember feeling bored in the middle of sex once. That is not the reaction of a typical 22 year old man.

Eventually, I started to describe myself as "Straight, but not very good at it". But even that didn't feel quite right. Calling myself "straight", even with a qualification, implied that I had some sort of heterosexual tendencies to speak of. I didn't. I saw sex all around me, but never had any desire to take part. I never looked at anyone and thought about getting it on with them. It had been years since I'd had sex, and it didn't bother me at all. Whenever my coworkers started talking about sex, it was like they were talking about a sport I didn't know how to play. I even thought that porn was dull and repetitive.

One day, I watched a sex scene in a TV show that ended up changing my life. Not because it was hot, not because it was erotic, or arousing, or passionately charged, or any of that stuff. It was because it made no sense at all to me. And that's when it struck me: I never looked at sex in the same way that *anyone* else around me ever had. Other people liked it. Wanted it. Craved it. Chased it. Thrived on it. I couldn't care less. That is not the reaction of a typical 31 year old man.

That incident made it perfectly clear that I was different and always had been different. I wasn't straight, because women weren't interesting to me. I wasn't gay, because men weren't interesting, either. I wasn't repressed. I wasn't religious. I'd never been abused. My equipment downstairs worked whenever I tested it. I wasn't showing any physical signs of a testosterone deficiency. So... What was going on? I went searching for an answer. It didn't take long to find one:

I was asexual.

Asexuality is a sexual orientation characterized by a persistent lack of sexual attraction toward any gender.

Well now, that was a bit of a dull and technical definition, but it's where I had to start. You see, that's really all asexuality is. Asexuality can be confusing, but if you just remember that definition, you'll be fine.

Most people are familiar with the concept of sexual orientation. Sexual orientation describes who a person is sexually attracted to. For instance, heterosexual people are attracted to people of the opposite gender, homosexual people are attracted to people of the same gender, and bisexual people are attracted to people of either gender.[1] Asexual people sort of fill in the gap in that list, and are not sexually attracted to anyone.

It's important to mention that sexual orientation does not describe behavior. It's possible for a heterosexual man to have had sex with other men because he was curious, and it's possible for a bisexual woman to be a virgin. Similarly, it's possible for an asexual to take part in sexual activity and still be asexual. It's about *attraction*, not *action*.

Like every other sexual orientation, asexuality is not a choice. We didn't just wake up one day and say "You know what, I'm tired of sex. I'm not going to feel attracted to anyone anymore." It's not celibacy or abstinence. Most of us will tell you that we were born like this, and many of us went through periods in our lives where we wondered why we were so different than everyone else.

---

[1] Then, of course, there's pansexuality and non-binary genders and all manner of other sexuality and gender identity related issues that would be impossible to enumerate here.

Asexuality is not a disease. It's not a medical condition. It's not caused by low hormones or a brain tumor. It's not a temporary phase. It's not the result of childhood trauma. It's not a response to a relationship gone wrong.

Asexuality is often misunderstood. Some people think that asexuality is the same as celibacy or abstinence. Others think that asexuality is a lack of (or a desire for a lack of) all sexual characteristics. Sometimes asexuality is described as a fear, avoidance, or hatred of sex, sometimes to the point of believing that asexuality is a religious or moral statement against people who have sex. And some people think that asexuality is a statement of a gender identity. None of these are true. I hope that this book will help to dispel some of these misconceptions.

Several studies have indicated that at least one percent of people are asexual. The famous Kinsey Report on sexuality in 1948 had a scale for one's sexual orientation, ranging from 0 for "exclusively heterosexual" to 6 for "exclusively homosexual". In his research, he found that some people (Around 1.5% of the adult male population) didn't really fit on the scale because they weren't particularly sexually interested in anyone, so he labeled them as "X" and left them off the scale. Today, this "X" group would likely be recognized as asexual.

A more recent study, conducted by Dr. Anthony Bogaert in 2004, found that approximately 1% of the adult population could be classified as asexual, using the results of a survey conducted in the UK during the 90s. However, Bogaert believed that the actual number of asexual people is likely higher, as it is conceivable that people who are not terribly interested in sex would be less likely to spend the time to take a survey about sex, and would therefore be underrepresented in the results.

There is no single "Asexual Experience". We are just as varied as everyone else. There are asexual women, asexual men, and asexuals of no particular gender. There are asexuals of every race and religion. We don't all vote the same way or watch the same TV shows. We don't all have extra ribs or pointy ears or stretchy rubber arms or glow under a UV lamp or anything like that. There's no secret dress code for asexuals. We don't all have black rings on our right middle fingers, black-grey-white-purple friendship bracelets, shirts that say "This is what an asexual looks like", or ace[2] flag bumper stickers on our cars.

It's impossible for a single book to capture the entire world of asexuality. My goal here is not to write the Encyclopedia of Aceness, but rather to write an introduction to asexuality. My target audience is anyone who wants to learn about asexuality, whether or not you're asexual.

---

[2] "Ace" is a colloquial abbreviation for "asexual". Many asexuals will use this term to refer to themselves or other asexual people. It's essentially the asexual equivalent of "gay" or "straight".

Common Questions About Asexuality

What is asexuality?

Asexuality is a sexual orientation. Unlike heterosexuality, where people are sexually attracted to the opposite sex, or homosexuality, where people are sexually attracted to the same sex, asexual people are not sexually attracted to anyone. It's not an inability to have sex, it's not celibacy or abstinence, it's not a temporary "dry spell", and it's not a fear of sex.

How do I become asexual?

Asexuality is not something you can switch on or off on a whim, asexuality is not a choice. Most asexual people will tell you that they've always been this way and that they've never known anything different. You can't become asexual any more than you can turn yourself gay or straight. Asexuality does not mean "not having sex". Certainly, you can practice abstinence and choose to become celibate, but asexuality and celibacy are not the same thing.

Can asexuals fall in love?

Although asexual people do not experience sexual attraction, that does not necessarily mean that they do not experience romantic emotions. As most people know, love does not equal sex, so it's possible to fall in love with someone and not be interested in having sex with them.

Can asexuals have children?

Asexuality has nothing to do with fertility. Asexual people are just as fertile and capable of producing offspring as non-asexual people. It still takes two, though. We're not capable of mitosis or budding or parthenogenesis or anything like that[3].

Can asexual men get erections?

Asexuality is not a physical condition. It's not a synonym for erectile dysfunction or impotence. Most asexual males have a fully operational penis that is capable of erection (as well as all of the other things the phrase "fully operational penis" implies).

Can asexuals masturbate?

For the most part, yes. Most asexual people have working parts downstairs, and that typically means that they are capable of self-stimulation and orgasm. There is nothing about asexuality that somehow prevents masturbation, and someone who masturbates is not somehow "disqualified" from being asexual.

However, just because we *can* doesn't mean that we all *do*. While many asexuals do masturbate, many do not.

Can asexuals have sex?

In general, yes, asexuals are physically capable of having sex. Asexuality is a sexual orientation and has no bearing on sexual ability. There are no physical characteristics inherent in asexuality. Asexual people typically have functioning genitalia which is indistinguishable from that of a non-asexual person. It is possible that an asexual person is physically unable to have sex, but if that is the case, then it is the result of some other condition and not the result of asexuality.

Now, that's not to say that asexual people necessarily *want* to have sex. Physical ability and willingness are two very different

---

[3] Although that sort of thing would be an awesome trick for parties.

concepts. Many asexuals, despite having functioning genitalia, have no interest in using that genitalia with anyone else.

How do I tell if someone is asexual?

You ask them.

There are no physical indicators of asexuality. You can't tell that someone is asexual just by looking, even if you're looking at them with their clothes off. You can't tell by how tall we are, by the rhythm to our step, by the way we talk, by the color of our eyes or by the size of our hair.

You can't look at the way someone behaves, either. Asexuals act the same as everyone else. You can't say "That person doesn't have sex, so they must be asexual", because being asexual doesn't necessarily mean that someone doesn't have sex, and not having sex doesn't necessarily mean that someone is asexual.

The only way to know for sure if someone is actually asexual is to talk to them about it.

Is there a cure for asexuality?

Asexuality is not a disease, so, no. There isn't a cure because there's nothing to be cured.

Is "asexual" another way to say "celibate"?

Celibacy and asexuality are not the same thing.

Celibacy is a behavior, it describes one's actions. A celibate person does not have sex.

Asexuality is an orientation, it describes one's attractions. An asexual person does not experience sexual attraction.

It's possible for a celibate person to experience sexual attraction and simply not act on it. It's possible for an asexual person to have sex, even though they don't feel any sexual attraction toward their partner. And it's possible for a person to be both celibate and asexual, where they don't have sex, nor do they experience sexual attraction.

How old does someone have to be before they can know they're asexual?

Old enough to say "I'm asexual".

There's no minimum age for asexuality, just like there's no minimum age for any other sexual orientation. You never hear anyone say "Well, you're only 15, so just to be safe, you might want to give it a few more years to see before you rule out bisexuality. You never know when some hot guy might catch your eye!" That would be ridiculous.

Presumably, by the time someone is at the point where they're comfortable with identifying as asexual, they've spent some time thinking about it. They've gone through the process of realizing that they're different from their friends and wondering why they're not as interested in sex as everyone else around them. They've spent long hard hours questioning themselves, trying to figure out who they are.

A lack of experiencing sexual attraction is the only thing that all asexuals have in common. That's what the definition of asexuality is. But that definition doesn't help people who are trying to figure out if they're asexual. It's a definition through negation, which isn't useful if you're not sure what's being negated. It's like saying "You're unxonoxian if you've never seen a xonox." How are you supposed to know if you've never seen a xonox, when you have absolutely no idea what a xonox is? Maybe you've seen one, but just didn't know that's what it was called. So you ask someone how to know if you've seen a xonox, and the best answer they can give is "Well, if you'd ever seen a xonox, *you'd know.*"[4]

Because of this, figuring out if you're asexual can be a challenge. How do you know if you've never felt sexual attraction when you're not sure what sexual attraction even is, and no one can satisfactorily explain it to you? What I've found is that most asexuals don't come to the realization that they're ace from reading the definition of the word. Instead, they read what someone else wrote on a blog or in forum posts, or they see a news article or YouTube video on asexuality and think, "That person is talking about *me.*"

Even though a lack of sexual attraction is the only thing all asexuals have in common, there are clusters of shared experiences, similar things that some asexuals have felt. It's these

---

[4] BTW, in case you're wondering, XONOX was a company that made uniquely-shaped double ended video game cartridges for the Atari 2600. It has absolutely no relation to asexuality, I just needed a nonsense word and that's what popped into my head, because that's just the kind of nerd I am.

shared experiences which often make people come to realize that they're asexual. In this section, I'm going to explore some of them.

(Please note: These aren't universal ace traits, so don't worry if you don't fit into them all. I haven't even experienced all of these myself. This shouldn't be looked at like a checklist or "Am I Asexual?" test or anything like that. You can still be asexual even if you've experienced none of the things on this list and you may not be asexual even if you've experienced most of them. There's no diagnostic test to confirm if you're asexual, there's no twenty-seven point checklist, and you don't have to pass an initiation or be referred by someone who's already in the club. The only person who can truly determine your sexual orientation is you.

Also, I want to note that these thoughts or experiences should not be taken as some sort of manifesto of the unquestioned and unified belief system of all asexuals. They're not necessarily the right experiences or the wrong experiences, and certainly, some of them may be misguided or born out of ignorance. I am writing about them here because some asexuals have passed through these thoughts on their way to discovering their identity, and I felt it was important to mention them for those people still making the journey and who may currently be thinking the same thoughts.)

In this first installment, I'm going to talk mostly about personal thoughts, thoughts about yourself and your identity.

You don't think about sex.

When thinking about activities you'd like to do with a romantic interest, sex rarely makes the list. You might not catch the punchline to a dirty joke, because you're not operating in that frame of reference. When other people start talking about sex, you have to take a second to remember that other people think about that sort of thing. When you hear that old statistic that people think about sex every seven seconds, you only think about how wrong that statistic is.

You realize that everyone else thinks about sex in a completely different manner than you do.

One day, I was talking with a friend about some sex scene on a TV show I'd seen the day before. I was trying to figure out the positioning and mechanics of what was supposedly going on because it didn't make sense to me. As the conversation went on, it became apparent that I was focused on the wrong thing, that it wasn't meant to be about the impossible and/or uncomfortable contortions required to make the scene believable, it was meant to be about the *sex*.

This, in itself, wasn't weird. I'll often find things odd about scenes in movies or TV shows and try to sort out the problems afterward. What was weird is that at no point in the conversation did I ever think anything like "Oh hey, sex! Yay!" I realized that I never really did think that way. *Ever.*

So I started rewinding my life, going over various sexual situations from my past. What struck me was how, in almost every single one of them, there was something that made me feel *different*. Left out. One or two things over the years might have just been a fluke. A handful of things bunched together during one summer might have just been a phase. But here, in event after encounter after situation, consistently, for close to 20 years since the start of puberty, there was something *different*.

I don't find people "hot".

My girlfriend had to be very persistent to convince me to have sex with her.

I find most porn to be boring or unappealing.

I zone out of most conversations about sex.

I never had "urges".

I never saw the point of a bachelor party.

And on and on the list went. It became absolutely clear to me that my views on sex were completely different from anyone else I'd ever talked to. It wasn't some isolated thing. There was something fundamentally *different* about me.

It was because of that realization that I went out to try to discover exactly what it was that was going on with me, which is how I discovered asexuality.

You think of sex in anthropological or scientific terms, rather than romantic or erotic terms.

You might be interested in sex, but interested in the same way one is interested in geology or zoology. You see it as an area of study, rather than an area of participation. You might want to know everything about it and read everything you can about sexual activities, practices, variants, and combinations, yet at the same time, you're not really interested in actually doing any of them. You'd rather watch a Discovery Channel documentary on sex than a porn movie. You'd rather read the Kinsey Report than Penthouse.

Sometimes, because of this, you may forget that others typically don't look at sex as an intellectual curiosity, and you may talk about things in a context where other people are shocked or embarrassed by your openness.

You don't understand what the big deal is. You haven't had sex for [insert significant amount of time here], so why are other people so worked up about going without for two weeks?

In general (although not universally speaking), asexual people don't have a problem going without sex for long periods of time. If you told an asexual person that they couldn't have sex for ten years, their response will often be something along the lines of "Okay, whatever." If you told a non-asexual person that, their response will often be something along the lines of "That's impossible! I'd explode!" (And again, not universally speaking.)

I've felt this way before. I've seen people moan about how terrible it is that they haven't had sex in two months. There was a big story about a DJ who went without sex for a whole year as a publicity stunt, and everyone was shocked. I've seen men make it sound like their genitals will literally explode under pressure if not emptied in, on, or by someone else within a timely manner. But I haven't had sex in years and I don't miss it at all. The concept that someone could be so affected by a lack of sex is totally alien to me.

So...

Sex is totally alien to you.

There's this *thing* that everyone else does. It's on TV, it's in movies, there are magazines devoted to it, songs about it, books about it. It's everywhere, all the time. Some people are obsessed by it. They can spend their whole lives chasing it, and sometimes it ruins them.

And you just don't get it at all.

It's not that you're naive, it's not that you're sheltered, it's not that you're uninformed. It's just that it's impossible to fathom why this *thing* is so important to pretty much everyone else in the world.

And whenever people talk about sex, they might as well be speaking in a foreign language or talking about the intricacies and nuances of macroeconomic theories or 17th Century French literature for all you care.

It's a bit like everyone else is a fan of a sport you're not interested in. You can watch a game, you can read the rules, you might even try playing once or twice, but in the end, it still doesn't make any sense why people are so excited about getting to third base or scoring a touchdown.

You've thought, "I'm straight (/gay/bi/etc.), but not very good at it".

I felt this way for years before I discovered asexuality. I'd had a girlfriend, and the occasional persons of vague interest had been women, so clearly that means I'm straight, right? But at the same time, I never really thought about sex. I never went looking for it, I never felt like I needed it. Whenever I thought about these women, I thought about things like going on vacation or scouring the local thrift stores for retro video games with them, but I never really thought about taking them to bed. One day, I decided that meant that I was straight, but I just wasn't very good at it.

Later, when I discovered asexuality, I mentioned this on an asexuality forum. I was surprised by the number of other people who said that they had felt the same way. Some of them had even used the same phrase to describe themselves.

You've thought, "I must be straight by default".

I've seen a couple of people say that they felt this way before they discovered asexuality. The assumption is that someone has to be straight, gay, or bi, no exceptions, no alternatives. Everyone has to get placed in one of those buckets, there are no other options. Clearly, since they didn't experience attraction to the same sex, they couldn't be gay or bi, therefore they had to be straight by default, since, through the process of elimination, that was the only bucket left.

I think this makes a good thought exercise for people who don't believe in asexuality. If those three groups are the only options, where do you put someone who knows they're not gay, because they're clearly not attracted to the same sex, but at the same time, there's not any evidence that they're straight, either? The only reason you'd put someone in the "straight" bucket is because "that's what most people are", which is a ridiculous reason to assign an identity to someone.

It's a bit like saying there are people who like chicken, people who like steak, and people who like both. You come across a vegetarian and you try to fit them into this limited worldview. "Do you like chicken?" *"No."* "Well, therefore you like steak by default." *"No, I'm-"* "You have to like steak, because most people like steak, and you said you don't like chicken." *"But-"* "YOU LIKE STEAK. END OF DISCUSSION." There's clearly a "none of the above" option here which needs to be recognized. Some people don't like steak or chicken, and some people don't like men or women.

Sex and Sexual Activities

In this second part, I'm going to talk about how you might view having sex and engaging in other sexual activities.

You'd much rather do X than do sex.

When you think about sex, you realize that there are dozens of things you'd much rather do. I'd rather read a book, I'd rather watch TV, I'd rather play a video game, I'd rather go to a movie, I'd rather stargaze, I'd rather walk the dog, I'd rather go shopping, I'd rather organize the books on the bookshelf by date of author's birth, I'd rather go bird watching, I'd rather build a Lego tribute to the Prime Ministers of Canada, I'd rather work on the car, I'd rather mow the lawn, I'd rather learn Esperanto, I'd rather fly a kite, I'd rather eat cake...

Your sex dreams don't really have sex.

I had a dream with a warning for "adult content and mature themes". It was about mortgage payments. I've had dreams where naked women throw themselves on me, and I tell them that I'm really busy and I'm supposed to be somewhere. I've had dreams where women are very obviously coming on to me, and I completely miss it. I've told women in dreams to put their clothes back on, because they look cold. It's like the part of my brain that generates dreams didn't get the memo that I'm asexual, so it's still sending out these prompts for sex dreams, but the rest of my brain doesn't process them, so they always end up weird.

Many asexuals say that they've never had sex dreams of any kind.

You think that "sexy" clothes just look uncomfortable or cold and can't understand why anyone would wear them.

Tight pants look like they're going to squeeze the life out of someone, and if it's a guy wearing them, you know he's gotta be in pain. Heels look like a broken ankle waiting to happen. Shirts that expose the midriff have to be freezing in this weather. All that lace is just going to leave a weird pattern in your skin. Thongs seem like they're going to cut you in half like a wire saw.

And I never got the point of make-up, either.

You don't really fantasize.

Everyone else seems like they undress people with their eyes.

Everyone else seems like they dream about having their way with the quarterback or the head cheerleader.

Everyone else seems like they would "hit that".

But not you. It's not that you *won't*, because you think it's sinful or something like that. It's that you *don't*. Your mind just doesn't work that way. It doesn't spontaneously imagine leaping into bed with someone. Maybe it's even that you *can't*. Maybe you've tried to devise erotic fantasies and have failed. You tried to undress someone with your eyes once, but you couldn't even figure out how to get their bra off. And if you can make it to the hot & heavy, rather than picturing the perfect mix of ecstasy and passion, you get bogged down in the details and end up distracted. You spend so much energy trying to maintain the fantasy that you lose whatever pleasure you were hoping to get from it.

You don't like sex.

Some asexuals don't like sex. They don't want to do it, they don't want to see it, they don't want to hear it, they don't want to think about it. At the age when most people were hearing about sex and thinking "I'd like to try that", they were thinking "You want me to do *what* with *WHAT*? No. Just. No."

While not liking sex doesn't necessarily mean one is asexual, many asexuals don't like sex and discover that they're asexual when they're trying to find out why they don't like sex.

A lot of non-asexual people feel this way, too, when they first hear about sex. Let's face it, the whole process is a bit icky, after all. However, for most people who feel this way, those thoughts are pushed aside once sexual attraction kicks in. But for the aversive asexual, sexual attraction never comes along to override these feelings.

The "ick factor" isn't the only reason people don't like sex. Some asexuals don't like sex because they find it uncomfortable or boring. There are thousands of reasons that someone might not like sex.

You like sex, but it doesn't feel "right".

I don't mean this in an "Oh, it's sinful and dirty" sense. I mean it in the sense where something seems off, like starting with the wrong hole when buttoning up a shirt or walking with gum on your shoe or using a shopping cart that always pulls to the right. At first glance, it seems like everything's okay, but the more you think about it, the more things feel off.

Perhaps you physically enjoy sex. Maybe you like making your partner feel good. There are things you might really like about sex, but at the same time, there's *something* missing. When you watch your partner's reactions, it's clear that there's something there that you're not feeling. It's impossible to put your finger on it, but you know there's something there. Some intangible spark is behind their eyes, and you're acutely aware that spark is missing in your eyes.

This was how I felt when I had sex. It physically felt great, but emotionally, I was not connected to the moment and to my partner. She wanted it, she was into it, she had been craving that moment for months, while I just didn't have any of that.

You had sex because that's what you were "supposed to do".

You never were really interested in having sex, you never felt a drive or biological desire to have sex, you never saw anyone and wanted to have sex with them, but you thought you wanted to have sex because "that's what people do". Later on, you got a partner, they wanted to have sex and you went along with it because "that's what people do". You kept having sex because "that's what I'm supposed to do". It felt more like an obligation or a chore than the expression of love it was supposed to be. At first, you may have even wanted the experience, but as time went on, you grew tired of it.

When you encountered the naked body of someone for the first time in a sexual situation, you looked at it like a real-life anatomy lesson, rather than an object of desire.

This one happened to me. I was in my bedroom with my first (and so far, only) girlfriend. Following her lead, we were fooling around a bit. She was wearing short shorts and sitting on my bed. She sat me down on the floor in front of her, spread open her legs, and pulled aside her shorts.

I think that most young men in this situation look upon it with unbridled glee. It's a milestone in their life, something they'd been working toward and dreaming about, often for years. Instantly, their mind fills with ideas and opportunities and a thousand fantasies, any number of which could come true within the next five minutes. For many men, a sight like that is like being invited into the playground of their dreams and told to run wild.

So, what went through my mind?

"Oh, so that's how it all fits together!"

There was no explosion of sexual urges, no endless stream of desires. I didn't really even feel compelled to touch anything. Instead, I was busy looking over the terrain like it was a road map, full of places I'd only heard of in passing. I wanted to identify all of the bits and pieces that I knew were supposed to be down there and see how they were all oriented relative to one another.

Needless to say, I now look at this event as one of the big red flags that should've clued me in that I was asexual years before I realized I was.

You focus on the motions, not emotions.

When dealing with sex and physical closeness, you put an emphasis on trying to make the right moves, like touching the right place in the right way, as if following a set of instructions, instead of focusing on the emotional aspects and going with the flow. In some cases, the pressure you feel to push all the right buttons may make the experience highly mechanical and unpleasant.

"If I try it, maybe I'll like it."

So, you haven't had sex. You're not terribly enthusiastic about it, either. It's not that you're against it, it's just not all that interesting to you. But everyone else seems to like it, so maybe you will too, if you just gave it a chance. Maybe you just need to try it out and you'll see what the fuss is about.

I call this the "Green Eggs and Ham" hypothesis:

You do not like them, so you say. Try them! Try them, and you may. Try them and you may, I say.

The idea that maybe you'll become interested in sex if you try it out is a compelling one. The thinking goes, how can you really know if you're not interested if you don't give it a shot? Well, the answer is that you really can know. After all, you don't actually have to hug a saguaro cactus to know that would be unpleasant. So, if you're certain that sex is not for you, then don't feel pressured to prove that you don't like it by going a few rounds.

On the other hand, if you feel this way and you're open to the experience and the right situation comes along, then go for it.

Maybe you'll like it, maybe you won't, it doesn't really matter either way. I felt this about myself, and I did try having sex. Of course, what it lead to was...

You had sex and thought "Is that it?"

That's it? That's all there is?

Weren't there supposed to be fireworks and standing ovations? Wasn't my life supposed to be changed forever? Wasn't it supposed to be the single greatest experience of my entire life?

What was supposed to be so great about that? Why do some people devote their entire lives to pursuing that? How could that possibly be responsible for ruining the careers of so many politicians? How could so many people consider that to be the very meaning of life?

I don't know, I guess it was kinda fun, a little bit, sorta. Bit boring, though, too.

I mean, seriously? Is that really it? What'd I miss?

Meh, whatever.

You don't like masturbating.

Maybe you've tried it before, but it didn't work out and you didn't get anywhere. Maybe you never saw the point. Maybe you do it, but you look at it like any other bodily function, like a sneeze or a shiver. Maybe you think it's gross or disgusting or repulsive. Maybe you do it and wish you could stop. In any case, you don't look at it as something pleasurable and fun. And it's not out of a sense of guilt or shame or anything like that. You just genuinely don't enjoy it.

You masturbate, so what would you need anyone else for?

You might look at other people and how they talk about sex and about what person X did for them last night, and think, "Huh, I can do that by myself. I don't need any help." You're perfectly fine taking care of yourself and really don't mind making reservations for sexual pleasure as a party of one. When other people talk about masturbation as if it were some sort of consolation prize for a distant runner up, you're a bit confused, because it certainly doesn't seem like a terrible thing to you.

When you think about having sex with someone else, you may think that a second person would just get in the way and complicate things. Maybe you've even had sex and didn't think that it was really any better than what you're capable of by yourself.

You think arousal is annoying.

Instead of looking at arousal as a sign from down below that you need to get all sexed up as soon as possible, you just find it annoying. It's distracting. It's random. And, for some people, it literally gets in the way. If you could shut it down, you would. It's never directed at anyone, you don't really want to do anything with it, it's just kinda *there*.

In this third section, I will talk about how you might view other people and their views on sex.

You've never wanted to "jump someone's bones". You've never thought "I'd hit that".

This is one of the more common reasons people discover that they're asexual. At some point in their lives, they'll look around and realize that other people say things like that and mean them. That straight out of the blue, one person will look at another, often a complete stranger, and think, "I would like to have sex with that person", and that, in some cases, this thought will drive people's actions.

Some asexuals may even look at this and think that's bizarre. Why would anyone do that sort of thing? The whole concept is so different from how they look at the same scenario that it may be impossible for them to process those kinds of thoughts into something that makes sense. For some asexual people, the thought "I would like to have sex with that person" could seem as random and unexpected as "I would like to paint that person blue, cover them with twigs, and dance around them in a circle all night".

You don't feel that anyone is "hot". "Cute", maybe, "pretty", maybe, but not "hot".

Some asexuals don't connect with the word "hot" or "sexy" and other words describing someone's sexual desirability. We're able to judge and rank subjective beauty on a scale from "ugly" to "pretty", we may feel that some people are "cute", but "hot" can be a word that some asexuals avoid. It's not that we don't *understand* it. We can usually point at someone and identify whether *other* people might classify them as "hot". It's that we don't *feel* it. When other people use words like "hot", we can sense that there's some innate internal buzzer going off inside their mind, and that the word is not just some synonym or sub-category of words like "cute" or "pretty". The word means more to them than "visually appealing". There's something behind it, some sense, some physical or emotional response that's driving them to choose "hot" over "pretty", and we don't experience what that sense is.

You thought that everyone else was just pretending to be interested in sex.

Many asexuals describe having a sort of "Emperor's New Clothes" view of sex at some point in their lives: That everyone else is just pretending to like sex simply because everyone else seems to like it, and they don't want to be the only one who speaks out and says "No, I'm not really into that." In this view, a sexually charged culture enforces conformity.

This view often comes about during the teenage years. The asexual's friends all start talking about boys or girls, but they don't feel anything yet themselves. Puberty strikes different people at different times and in different ways, so at first, they'll just think they're not there yet, but as time goes on, they'll realize that they never started getting all that interested in boys or girls. This may lead to thoughts like, "Well, I never got interested in sex, so maybe no one else really did, either. Maybe they're all just faking to fit in."

Which brings us to...

You just pretended to be interested in sex.

Sometimes, some asexuals will feel pressured to pretend to be interested in sex in order to fit in. All your friends get caught up in what they'd like to do and who they'd like to do it with, but you don't feel that way about anyone. So, you just smile and nod, until...

"So, who do YOU like?"

...and you sputter out something about Johnny or Sally, not because you're actually interested in them, but because they seemed like acceptable options to use to hide how you really feel, because if you told your friends how you really feel, they'd just laugh at you and think you're a freak.

And so, you lie and go along with it. Eventually, you may even end up in a relationship and...

You pretended to like sex so your partner wouldn't think you didn't love them.

For many people, love and sex are inextricably linked. A sexual rejection is taken as a rejection of the person as a whole, a sign that they're unloved, rather than just an indication that their partner has an activity they're not all that interested in. This can pose a challenge for asexuals in a relationship. They can be truly, madly, deeply, and endlessly in love, yet just not care for sex. They fear that letting their partner know how they feel would mean that their love would be doubted and the relationship would be destroyed as a result. "If you *really* loved me, you'd want sex with me."

It's even possible that the asexual partner does enjoy sex, but are afraid to let their partner know that they don't find them sexually attractive. And so, they put on an act of attraction and will say things like "You're so hot" or "You turn me on so much" when that's not actually the case.

Sex is not love, love is not sex. It's possible to love someone you're not sexually attracted to. It's possible to have and even enjoy sex, even if you're not sexually attracted to the person you're involved with.

Conversations about sex aren't interesting.

Friends and coworkers like to talk about sex. They like to talk about what they've done, what they'd like to do, and what they've heard about other people doing. They boast about bachelor(ette) parties or one night stands. They discuss who's hot, how hot they are, and what attributes make them hot. They make suggestive comments about the delivery person or the receptionist or the wait staff at the restaurant.

And you couldn't care less.

If they're talking about other people, like how "hot" the waitress is or how "steamy" the delivery guy is, there's a good chance that you didn't even notice the person until someone pointed them out. If they're talking about parties or one-night stands, there's a good chance you don't have any comparable experiences to discuss. You just zone out when they start talking about these things, and let the conversation run its course. Sometimes, people may notice that you've gone quiet and think that you're offended by where the conversation has gone, but that's not necessarily the case. You've gone quiet because you've got no input, no commentary, no questions.

You often find sex scenes in books/TV/movies to be out of place or boring.

You're watching a movie when suddenly the male and female leads start going at it for no reason: *[fast forward!]*

You're reading a book when suddenly it turns to "heaving bosoms" and "love's juices": *[next chapter!]*

Perhaps it's a sense of "Ew, icky", but it doesn't have to be. More often, it's a sense of "Why are they doing that? What's the point? Get back to the story!" Half the time, the sexual encounter is unforgivably contrived. Sometimes you can even imagine the writers meeting with their editor or producer and being told to "sex it up a bit, the ratings are off this year", and the writers just randomly drawing character names from a hat to decide who should go at it.

Bad acting and lame stories in porn really bug you, because, after all, what's the point in watching a movie if it's no good?

"Oh, come on, if that sort of thing happened in real life, she'd have that doctor arrested. That guy is a terrible actor, it's like he never even bothered to look at the script. And don't even get me started on that set and how cheap it looks! It's supposed to be a doctor's office, so where's the blood pressure thingy and the jar of tongue depressors and the bed with the paper stuff? I mean, that looks like a cheap Army surplus cot from the 50's! That can't possibly be sterile! What's this now? Why is she moaning? He's not anywhere near her! What is supposed to be happening? She keeps looking directly at the camera, too. And that guy keeps getting in the way of the shot. Didn't the director plan out the scene with the actors ahead of time? *Why am I even watching this?*"

You feel like sex comes naturally to everyone else, but you have to work at it.

You look at other people, and they seem to instinctively understand sex, and how to play the game. Your partner handles it effortlessly, while for you, sex ends up more like a poorly-choreographed attempt at a secret handshake that no one taught you than a spontaneous expression of intimacy. It's like everyone else went to some sort of intensive training camp and knows everything inside and out, while you have to pick it up on the job. Even so, there's some secret that everyone else seems to know, the key to understanding the whole thing, and you know that you will never learn that secret, no matter how hard you try.

If given the hypothetical chance of a no-strings, no-regrets, no-consequences sexual encounter, you'd have to think about it.

Usually, this comes in the form of a hypothetical situation: "Random Hot Person X appears in front of you and says 'Let's get it on'. Would you go for it?" For many people, the response is an unequivocal and immediate, "Yes". For others, it's "No, I can't, my boyfriend wouldn't let me". But for you, it's something more like, "Well, I don't know... It's Friday. Fringe is on. I guess I could record it, but I was looking forward to watching it all day."

You never initiate sex.

It's not that you dislike sex. It's not that your partner isn't any good. It's that you just never think about it. It's never on your mind. So, as a result, you never think, "Hey, I'd like to have sex right now. I should go see if my partner is up for it."

This, of course, can cause problems in relationships. Your partner may end up feeling like they always do all the work and may even begin to think that your lack of initiative is an indication that you're not really in love with them.

You don't catch it when people are flirting, even when you're the one doing the flirting.

I've seen this one pop up in asexual discussions a couple of times. It's happened to me, and I just thought I was completely oblivious. I've been told that I'm good at flirting, even though I just thought I was having a normal conversation. And whenever someone is flirting with me, I won't notice. (And probably wouldn't know what to do, even if I did.) Only hours later, when I think back on the conversation, will I realize that something was off.

I was once on vacation, in a park, taking 3D pictures with a homemade stereoscopic camera. A woman called me over and started asking questions about the camera, and telling me how she was a photographer, too. We spoke for a minute or two, then I continued wandering around the park. On my way back to my car, I passed the bench, and she loudly lamented to her friend "Where are all the good men in this town?"

I was literally *in the next state* when I realized that she probably wasn't *that* interested in my camera.

Asexuality: Myths, Misconceptions and Other Things That Are Just Plain Wrong

Since asexuality is rather unknown, it is subject to a lot of misinformation and ignorance. Many of these misconceptions can be offensive and hurtful. All of these are things that people have actually said to or about asexual people. It's time to set the record straight.

Asexuals don't exist.

I'm asexual. I wrote this. You're reading this. Therefore this exists, therefore I exist, therefore asexuals exist.

QED.

Asexuality is the same as celibacy.

Asexuality describes someone's *sexual orientation*, that is, that they do not experience sexual attraction to anyone. Celibacy describes someone's *behavior*, that is, that they do not have sex with anyone. Orientation is not behavior, attraction is not action. Celibacy and asexuality are neither mutually exclusive nor mutually linked. It is possible for an asexual person to not have sex and be celibate, and it's also possible for an asexual to have sex and not be celibate.

I do consider myself to be celibate, as I have not engaged in any sexual activity with anyone else in over nine years.

Asexuality is a choice.

Asexuality is not a choice. It is a sexual orientation, like heterosexuality or homosexuality, and like those orientations, it cannot be turned on or off on a whim.

I never woke up one morning, thinking, "You know, I'm tired of being turned on by people. I think I'm going to stop that now." I've always been this way.

Asexual people can't fall in love.

Many asexuals can feel the full range of romantic emotions, from a slight crush to true love. It's just devoid of a sexual component. Asexuals are not limited to platonic love, either. When an ace feels love, it can be every bit as complex and deep as the romantic love that anyone else feels.

There is a concept of romantic (or affectional) orientation, which describes who a person is romantically attracted to. Romantic orientation is separate from sexual orientation, although in many people, their romantic and sexual orientations do happen to coincide. Common romantic orientations include heteroromantic (romantic attraction toward the opposite gender), homoromantic (romantic attraction toward the same gender), bi/panromantic (romantic attraction toward both/all genders), and aromantic (no romantic attraction toward any gender).

Asexual people don't/can't have sex.

Most asexual people can have sex, and some of them do. I have. Asexuality is the lack of sexual attraction, not a lack of sexual ability. Asexuals are physically and physiologically indistinguishable from other people, in other words, in most cases, the equipment is all there and in working order. If an asexual person is incapable of having sex, it is usually due to some other condition, and not necessarily related to their asexuality.

Asexuality is just a phase that you'll grow out of.

I'm 32 and have never been sexually attracted to anyone, not even a naked woman standing in front of me, touching my junk and inviting me to reciprocate. How exactly can that be considered a "phase"? When am I going to grow out of it?

It's just a hormone problem.

Most asexuals have hormones within normal ranges. Asexuals who have started taking hormone supplements for some reason have reported no change in their orientation.

That's not what "asexual" means.

And "gay" only means "happy" and "straight" only means "not curved". Words in the English language can have multiple meanings and can change over time. Deal with it.

Getting laid will fix that.

First of all, there's nothing to fix because we're not broken. Secondly, no, no it won't. I was asexual before I had sex and I'm still asexual now. Many other aces who've had sex have had the same experience. Sex wasn't some super-awesome life-changing milestone that upended my worldview.

The corollary to this misconception is "Getting laid *by me* will fix that", which ranks somewhere up around "Know what'd look good on you? Me." on the list of dumbest ideas ever for pickup lines.

You can't know for sure unless you've had sex.

You don't have to have sex to know what your sexual orientation is. Most people, when they proceed into puberty (and in some cases, even before then), will naturally start to feel attracted to other people without having to engage in any kind of sexual activity at all. They'll know that they're straight or gay or bi or what have you and they typically don't have to hold try-outs to know which team they play for. Asexual people are the same way.

They'll know that they don't feel that spark of sexual attraction, that they're somehow not straight or not gay, that they're different from everyone else, and they don't need to have sex to confirm it.

I'm virtually certain that had I known what asexuality was before I had sex, I would have identified that way without needing sex to be certain. As it was, I didn't learn about asexuality for years after I had sex, but I knew that I was different.

Asexual people don't/can't masturbate.

In general, asexuals can masturbate and many do. Asexuals generally don't have impaired genital function, which means the parts typically work, and when the parts work, they can feel good to use. Aces who masturbate will do so for reasons ranging from relieving tension to wanting the pleasure of an orgasm. Of course, masturbation is a personal choice, and while many asexual people will masturbate, many do not.

I masturbate fairly regularly.

All asexuals are virgins.

Nope, sorry. I had my v-card punched years ago. Many other asexuals have also had sex. Some have regular sexual partners, some are parents. There's no virginity requirement for being asexual, just as there's no loss of virginity requirement for being heterosexual.

Asexuals are hermaphrodites.

Being intersex is completely unrelated to asexuality. The various conditions grouped under the umbrella of "intersex" are all physical conditions. Asexuality is not physical. However, it is possible for an intersex person to be asexual.

(By the way, the word "hermaphrodite" is generally considered offensive, so don't say that.)

Asexuality is the same as being a transsexual or transgender.

Asexuality is not a gender identity issue. Most aces are cis-gendered, but some are trans, others are agendered, genderfluid, or what have you. Asexuality only describes who someone is sexually attracted to (namely, no one), and has nothing to do with the gender they are.

I happen to be a cis-gendered male.

Asexuals just haven't met the right person yet.

This assertion offends many asexuals. They've seen thousands upon thousands of people in their life and have not been sexually attracted to any of them. This claim acts to invalidate and deny a part of their core identity. It's a bit like going up to a heterosexual male and saying "You could really be gay, you know. Maybe you just haven't met the right man yet. Keep trying, you'll find him someday."

Everyone feels like that sometimes.

I know that non-asexual people don't walk around in an endless horny cloud of lust all day, every day, and that everyone feels like this *sometimes*. But I feel like this *all the time*. I've never found anyone attractive. I don't know what it's like to think that someone's hot. I've never passed a woman on the street and had my mind start turning through all the things I'd like to do with her in bed. I don't relate to the manifestations of sexual attraction that I see around me every day.

Ever.

And that's what makes me different. That's what makes me asexual.

Asexuals are really just gays in denial.

Homosexual people are sexually attracted toward people of the same sex. Asexual people are not sexually attracted to either sex. Asexual people are not hiding their attraction, they simply do not have any attraction to hide.

I have never felt any attraction, sexual or romantic, toward other men.

Asexual people are just afraid of sex or are disgusted by sex.

Some asexuals are afraid of or are disgusted by sex. Some non-asexual people are, too. Such feelings are not tied to one's sexual orientation. There are also many asexuals who don't mind sex. They've had sex or are open to the idea of having sex in the right situation. I'm in this latter group. I've done it before and I'd be willing to do it again in the right situation.

Asexual people are victims of some sexual trauma in their past.

The vast majority of asexual people have never had any kind of sexual trauma. Most asexuals will be highly offended by someone trying to pin their lack of sexual attraction on some sort of unspoken, possibly repressed event. And if they are victims of some past trauma, they're generally not going to appreciate it when you bring it up and try to use it to invalidate their identity.

They have a pill that'll fix that.

They have pills that'll fix physical ailments, such as hormonal imbalances or blood flow issues. Asexuality is not a physical ailment. There's no pill that'll make an asexual start experiencing sexual attraction. It would be like there being a pill that would turn a gay person straight.

Asexuality is caused by a brain tumor.

Hour-long medical procedural TV shows should not be considered reliable sources regarding sexual orientations. Moving on...

Asexuals don't/can't have orgasms.

The majority of asexuals have typical, fully functioning sexual organs. This means that the majority of asexuals have the capacity to orgasm. Many asexuals do have orgasms, and often enjoy them. Certainly not all asexuals have had orgasms, and some do not have fully functioning sexual organs, however, those cases are not due to asexuality. Asexuality is only a description of sexual orientation, and in no way attempts to describe sexual ability.

I do have orgasms and I like them.

Asexuals are all homophobes.

This is categorically false. The vast majority of asexuals are LGBT+ friendly. There is absolutely nothing inherent in asexuality that minimizes, dismisses, invalidates, passes judgment on, or attacks homosexuality in any way. Asexuality is another sexual orientation that coexists alongside every other sexual orientation.

Asexuals are all super-religious and against sex.

Asexuality has nothing to do with one's religious beliefs. Asexuality is not a form of abstinence, it's not the result of a purity pledge, and it's not that we're "saving ourselves". It's equally possible for an asexual person to be a hardcore born-again no-sex-til-marriage brand of Christian as it is for an asexual person to be an atheist who enjoys casual sex with strangers on the weekends.

Asexuals all hate sex and everyone who has sex.

Asexuality should not be confused with antisexuality. Most asexuals have no problem with sex. Some don't like the idea of sex when it comes to themselves, but are typically indifferent when it comes to other people. Some even enjoy having sex. Asexuality is merely a sexual orientation, it doesn't have any effect one's opinion on sexual activity.

I actually kinda liked sex. It was a bit boring, but at least it felt good.

Asexuals are naïve and don't know anything about sex.

Asexuality is not somehow a function of a lack of information about sex. There are plenty of people out there who know very little about sex besides what goes where, and they're not all asexual. Conversely, there are plenty of asexuals who know quite a bit about sex and sexual practices, even though they're not necessarily all that interested in trying them out.

I happen to have a rather sizable library on the various facets of human sexuality, from textbooks and research papers to illustrated sex manuals. I have a bit of an anthropological curiosity on the subject, probably from my repeated attempts to figure out where I fit.

Asexuals are just faking it for attention.

How is someone who's in the closet and agonizing over their identity "faking it for attention"? Most aces are in the closet or are not very open about it precisely because they fear the sort of attention they'll get. All of these things in this list are actual things that people have said to asexual people.

Certainly, there are some people who will claim to be asexual because it's trendy. But there are also people who pretend to be gay for some reason, and no one tries to use them as evidence that disproves the existence of homosexuality in its entirety.

In real life, I hardly ever mention that I'm asexual, as it's not typically relevant to the day-to-day experience of a software engineer. The most attention I've gotten from it have been a few awkward (yet positive) conversations with my parents and a guy at work saying "Yeah, we all kinda figured that." So *clearly*, that's what I'm going for with this.

There are no asexual men.

There aren't? Man, and I was so sure that I existed, too... Do I have to take back my "QED"?

Asexual men do exist, contrary to the stereotypes. I'm one of them. David Jay is, as well. He's one of the most prominent asexual visibility activists around. He founded AVEN, the Asexual Visibility and Education Network, the largest asexual community on the Internet. Perhaps you've heard of it?

And we're far from the only two around.

Asexuality is a moral stand against sex.

Asexuality is nothing more than a sexual orientation. It's not inherently for or against sex or people who have sex. When an asexual says something like "I don't look at people that way" or "I don't understand why people think sex is so important", it's not a value judgment, it's not an attack. It's just a statement of fact. They literally don't feel that way, they don't understand it.

It's also worth repeating that asexuality is not a choice, so it can't be a decision that one makes to stand against anything.

Asexuality is evolution's response to overpopulation.

I've seen this idea come up several times. There are so many things wrong with this idea that I don't know where to begin... The concept of "overpopulation" is one of sustainability, not of actual, physical, overpopulation. I have plenty to eat and plenty of space to live in, as did my parents when I was born. Evolution didn't come by one day and say "Well, there's famine thousands of miles away in Africa right now and if you project out the current growth rates and consumption trends, there's gonna be problems everywhere in about a hundred years, so, you know what? I think I'm gonna make you not be interested in women." That's just not how evolution works. There's the whole bit where advantageous traits are passed along throughout the generations, because they assist in successful reproduction, even if indirectly. If there's a trait that makes an organism not interested in reproduction, then that trait doesn't get passed on, so it can't become common within a population.[5]

If evolution actually were responding to overpopulation, it would probably just make us smaller so we consume less. Evolution typically doesn't get much of a chance to respond to overpopulation, though, because famine and disease are far more effective instruments of population control which can eliminate the problem in a single generation.

Asexuals are all just confused teenage girls.

My driver's license disagrees with this statement on multiple counts. Many asexuals are not teenagers. Many asexuals are not girls. And even those asexuals who are teenage girls tend not to be confused. Most people who identify as asexual do not do so on a whim or because we somehow just can't recognize what sexual attraction is. An asexual person generally examines their life very carefully before coming out, so you can be fairly certain that when

---

[5] On top of that, it doesn't really matter if something was done to lower my effective fertility, since there's plenty of people with reality TV shows that are more than making up for me.

someone says "I'm asexual", the last thing they are is confused about how they feel.

You're just single and looking for an excuse for why you're afraid to date.

Except for those asexuals who aren't single, or who genuinely don't care about dating, or who really wouldn't mind dating if the right person came along...

Asexuals hate their gender.

Asexuality has nothing to do with gender identity. There are male asexuals and female asexuals and transgender asexuals and cisgender asexuals and agender asexuals and genderqueer asexuals and neutrois asexuals and all sorts of other gender asexuals that I haven't mentioned here. Some of them dislike their gender, some of them are happy with it, and some of them don't care. And none of them are the gender they are because they're asexual and none of them are asexual because of the gender they are.

Things That Are Not Asexuality

Asexuality is a sexual orientation where a person does not experience sexual attraction. That's all it is. However, since asexuality isn't well known, it's often confused with similar (and sometimes not even remotely similar) concepts. Because of this, it's important to point out these distinctions and differences. It's also important to note that most of these concepts are not necessarily mutually exclusive with asexuality. For instance, even though asexuality is not celibacy, it's possible for someone who is asexual to also be celibate.

Asexuality is not celibacy or abstinence.
Celibacy and abstinence describe behavior, they're about actions. A celibate or abstinent person does not have sex. Asexuality is an orientation, it's about attraction, not action. An asexual person does not experience sexual attraction, but they may or may not have sex.

Asexuality is not a lack of sexuality.
Asexuality doesn't mean that someone can't have sex. Asexuality doesn't mean that someone can't masturbate. Asexuality doesn't mean that someone can't wear make-up or nice clothes. Asexuality doesn't mean that someone can't be interested in sex. Asexuality doesn't mean that someone is infertile or impotent. Asexuality doesn't mean that someone doesn't have a libido. Asexuality means that someone doesn't experience sexual attraction, and that's all.

Asexuality is not virginity.
Asexuals do not experience sexual attraction, and won't suddenly start experiencing sexual attraction by having sex. Many asexuals have had sex, and yet are still asexual. In fact, many

asexuals don't even discover that they're asexual until after they've had sex and start to wonder why they're not all that interested in it.

Asexuality is not a hormone imbalance.

Many asexuals have had their hormones tested and have found them to be within normal levels. Some asexuals have undergone hormone therapy for other conditions and have not reported any change in their sexual orientation. In general, asexual people do not experience any of the other signs of a hormone imbalance (hair loss, erectile dysfunction, depression, hot flashes, etc.), so even when they haven't been specifically tested, they can be reasonably sure that their hormones are in order. Also, a loss of sexual interest due to a hormone imbalance is often sudden, while an asexual person typically has never experienced sexual attraction for their entire lives, so it's not like anything was "lost", because it was never there.

(If you do have reason to believe that your hormones may not be in order, particularly if you've suddenly lost the interest in sex that you used to have, go see a doctor about it.)

Asexuality is not a fear of sex.

Being asexual doesn't mean someone afraid of sex, just like being heterosexual or homosexual doesn't mean a person loves sex. Being asexual doesn't say anything about a person's opinion of sex. Some asexuals are afraid of sex. Some asexuals love sex. Some asexuals are indifferent to sex. Many people who do experience sexual attraction are afraid of sex, but that does not make them asexual.

Asexuality is not a purity pledge or a religious act.

Asexuality has nothing to do with adhering to religious beliefs and is not the result of taking a purity pledge. If one chooses not to have sex because their religion or personal beliefs prohibit it, that's abstinence, not asexuality. It is possible for someone who is asexual to refrain from sexual activity for religious reasons, which would make them abstinent and asexual. On the flip side, there are many asexuals who are not religious and do not appreciate having religious motivations ascribed to them.

Asexuality is not a choice.

Like every other sexual orientation, asexuals were born this way. We never looked at our lives one day and thought "You know, I'm done with this sex stuff" and decided to become asexual. You cannot choose to be asexual any more than you can choose to be gay or straight. Certainly, you can choose who you have sex with or whether or not you have sex at all, but that's behavior, not who you're attracted to. If you experience sexual attraction and choose not to act on it, then you're not asexual. Asexual people do not experience sexual attraction.

Asexuality is not a disease.

There's nothing physically wrong with people who are asexual. We're not asexual because of a tumor or a virus or a parasite. We're not contagious. Some people like men, some people like women, some people like both, some people don't care, and there's nothing to cure about any of those cases.

Asexuality is not sexual immaturity.

Someone who is asexual isn't asexual because they've never had sex or haven't had enough sex. Someone who is asexual isn't asexual because they haven't met the right person yet. Someone who is asexual isn't asexual because they're hiding or repressing their sexual desires. Someone who is asexual isn't asexual because they're in some perpetual state of child-like naivete. Someone who is asexual is asexual because they don't experience sexual attraction. No amount of experience or information is going to change that.

Asexuality is not a physical condition.

There are no physical signs of asexuality. Just like you can't tell if someone is straight or gay or pan or bi just by looking at them, you can't tell someone is asexual just by looking at them. Being asexual doesn't mean that something downstairs doesn't work right. Being asexual doesn't mean that someone has no genitals.

Asexuality is not a lack of libido.

Libido is also known as a "sex drive", that is, the desire or impulse to experience sexual satisfaction. Some asexuals do have a libido, it's just that it's essentially aimless. Their bits downstairs will activate and call out for attention, but that doesn't make a person feel sexually attracted toward anyone else.

Asexuality is not a gender identity.

Asexuality has nothing to do with someone's gender. There are asexual men, asexual women, asexuals who are transgender, and asexuals of no gender. Asexuality does not mean someone is unhappy or uncomfortable with their gender or the parts they were born with. Asexuality does not mean that a person is genderless.

Asexuality is not a relationship status.

On places like Tumblr and Twitter, I've seen many people say things like "Boys suck, I'm turning asexual now". Asexuality is a sexual orientation, it doesn't mean that you're avoiding sex because of a bad relationship experience. If someone is avoiding sex, that's called celibacy or abstinence, not asexuality. You can't be temporarily asexual because of a bad break up, that's just not how it works.

Asexuality is not a relationship cure-all.

Similar to the "Boys suck, I'm asexual" line, I've seen people say things like "I wish I were asexual, then I wouldn't have any problems." Asexuality does not mean that someone does not participate in romantic or sexual relationships. Many asexuals will end up in relationships, and those relationships can have just as many problems as relationships between non-asexual people. In fact, if an asexual ends up in a relationship with a non-asexual person, that can lead to all sorts of problems due to mismatched sexual interest.

Asexuality is not a dry spell.

If someone hasn't had sex for a week, that doesn't make them asexual. If someone hasn't had sex for a month, that doesn't make them asexual. If someone hasn't had sex for a year, that doesn't make them asexual. If someone hasn't had sex for a decade, that doesn't make them asexual. There isn't some span of time that someone has to go without sex before they're granted the title of asexual, because that's not what asexuality is. Asexuality is about not experiencing sexual attraction, not a lack of sex.

Symbols of Asexuality

The Asexuality Flag

The Asexuality Flag (also called the "Ace Flag") is made up of four equally sized horizontal stripes. From top to bottom, the colors are black, grey, white, and purple.

The need for a flag was driven primarily by the desire to have a symbol that belongs to all of us, something that we could use to identify as ace and represent asexuality with that was not tied to a specific group. Prior to its adoption, people would use things like the AVEN triangle or a half-filled heart, but those had problems which prevented their wider adoption. The AVEN triangle is, well, the *AVEN* triangle. It's the logo of a single website that not every asexual person is affiliated with. The half-filled heart implies romance, which meant that many aromantics were uncomfortable using it.

In the Summer of 2010, a number of asexuality sites, led by users on AVEN, came up with a number of designs for an asexuality flag, then held a multi-stage vote to determine the winner. The selected design was created by AVEN user standup, and first posted at 4:36 PM on June 30th, 2010.

Some of the other designs included hearts and spades and triangles and all manner of other symbols. Some of the designs looked like country flags. In the end, the simple, four-bar design was chosen. This design avoids the unwanted connotations that specific symbols like a triangle or heart might have, it avoids any hint of national affiliation, and perhaps most importantly, it fits in with the striped designs of most other GSM pride flags.

(Plus, it's really easy to draw.)

The four colors all have meanings:
Black: Asexuality.

Grey: Grey-Asexuality and Demisexuality.
White: Non-asexual partners and allies.
Purple: Community.

Since the flag was selected in 2010, its use has exploded. You can get buttons and bumper stickers and clothes with the flag on it. It's been seen at pride parades around the world, and some flag makers now offer it for sale. Many asexuality related websites or blogs now incorporate the flag into their design. And, of course, people have even made ace flag cakes. Additionally, the black-grey-white-purple color scheme has been adopted by many aces as a way of indicating their asexuality. I've seen ace shirts, ace nail polish, ace friendship bracelets, ace headbands, and ace scarves. Even the cover of this book incorporates these four colors.

The flag first appeared in this post:
http://www.asexuality.org/en/index.php?/topic/51646-asexual-flag-thread/page__view__findpost__p__1571308

Black Rings

Some people will wear a black ring on the middle finger on their right hand in order to signify that they are asexual. There's no particular significance to the color or finger selection. Black was chosen because it was a neutral color, while the right middle finger was chosen largely because a ring on the left middle finger would clash with a wedding band or engagement ring on the left.

Most of the time, the ring is a plain black band of some sort, made out of plastic, stainless steel, or hematite. Some people will opt for a fancier design, with an "Ace" symbol, or with purple and grey highlights.

The black ring symbol began in a thread on AVEN in June of 2005:

http://www.asexuality.org/en/index.php?/topic/9175-show-your-pride/

Cake

At some point, you may notice that some groups of asexuals seem to have a strange obsession with cake. This isn't because asexuals are all secretly bakers. Rather, it's because cake is clearly better than sex, something that asexuals and non-asexuals can agree on.

Some factions of asexual people have the view that pie is, in fact, even better than cake, while others claim this belief is heretical. A tense truce has existed between the two sides ever since the Confectionery Crisis of 2007. This author refuses to take sides in this debate[6], and believes that any choice is the right one (including both or neither), as long as you're walking your own personal path of truth.

---

[6] Although CLEARLY, cake is better. I mean, seriously, *pie*? Come on!

So, you're asexual. That means you can't love anyone and are going to die alone, right?

Asexuality only means that a person does not experience sexual attraction. It doesn't mean that they can't fall in love. It doesn't mean that they want to be alone forever. It just means that they don't see someone and immediately want to jump their bones. There have been asexual people who have fallen in love and gotten married.

Wait, so... Some asexuals get married? What do they do on the honeymoon?

Play Scrabble.

(No, really[7].)

But how can you fall in love with someone and not want to have sex with them?

Love and sex are different things. Appreciation of beauty and sex are different things. It is quite possible to think someone is stunningly gorgeous and be dumb-struck in love with them and not be interested in having sex with them.

There's a word for a relationship without sex. It's "Friendship".

There are many non-asexual couples where the sexual flame has long been extinguished, but who are still inseparable. There are many non-asexual couples who are in circumstances where they can't have sex, but they're still madly in love. Just because

---

[7]http://www.guardian.co.uk/lifeandstyle/2008/sep/08/relationships.healthandwellbeing

there's no sex, that doesn't negate the romantic aspect of the relationship. Would you say to an elderly couple that they're "just friends" because he's no longer able to perform? Would you tell a couple who've been in a bad car accident that they're "just friends" because she's paralyzed?

But those people are still attracted to each other. How can you have a relationship without attraction?

There are actually multiple different kinds of attraction. Sexual attraction is just one. Asexuals don't experience sexual attraction, however, they may experience other types of attraction. Romantic attraction is what draws a person toward someone else and makes them want to get into a relationship with that person. For most people, romantic attraction and sexual attraction are directed toward the same person. They will find someone romantically and sexually attractive, that is, they will want to have a relationship with that person and they'll want to include sex as part of that relationship.

It's possible to experience sexual attraction without romantic attraction. A one-night stand, a friends-with-benefits situation, even some extramarital affairs are often examples of this arrangement. A person will only see the partner as sexually interesting, but not want to become romantically involved.

For many asexuals, they will experience romantic attraction without sexual attraction. They'll want a girlfriend or boyfriend, and want to do most of the things that couples do, like go on dates, live together, take trips with each other, even get married, file joint income tax returns, and spend every moment of the rest of their lives together. But amongst all of that, there's no burning desire to do the horizontal mambo. And it's not a temporary "Not tonight dear, I have a headache" type of thing. The interest just isn't there.

How do asexuals find a partner? Do they just randomly pick someone out of the phone book and call them up for a date?

Um. No.

Just like the different sexual orientations you're probably already familiar with, there are multiple romantic orientations:

Heteroromantic: Romantically attracted to the opposite sex/gender.

Homoromantic: Romantically attracted to the same sex/gender.

Biromantic/Panromantic: Romantically attracted to both/all sexes/genders.

Aromantic: Romantically attracted to no one.

For instance, a heteroromantic man would be interested in a romantic relationship with women. Likewise, a homoromantic woman would be interested in having a relationship with other women.

In some cases, a heteroromantic asexual might call themselves a "straight asexual" or a homoromantic ace might say they're a "gay asexual" or "asexual lesbian". Those terms are used as convenient shorthand, because words like "heteroromantic" are a mouthful and tend to get confused blank stares from other people. However, other asexuals will refuse to use those words to describe themselves, as they carry such a strong sexual connotation.

In my case, I lie somewhere between heteroromantic and aromantic and I still haven't quite sorted it out yet. I know that I'm not homo- or bi-romantic because I've never felt any interest in having a relationship with a man. But at the same time, I'm not terribly drawn into wanting a relationship with a woman, either. I had a girlfriend once, but it never felt quite right. Whenever I think about being in a relationship, I don't desire closeness or inseparability. It's more that I want someone who'll take the wheel on long road trips or run interference against salespeople in the store or help me load Ikea furniture into the car. But I know that I'd want it to be a woman. So yeah, still totally confused there... Moving on.

In addition to romantic attraction, there's aesthetic attraction. Aesthetic attraction, aside from being remarkably troublesome to spell, is being attracted to the way someone looks. This may sound sexual in nature, but it is not. Instead of thinking, "He's hot, I'd totally tap that", aesthetic attraction is more along the lines of "He's cute, I'd totally stare at him for hours and study the lines and curves and contours and the interaction of the lighting on his hair and the way the colors he is wearing highlight his fingernails". It's more like the sense one gets looking at a beautiful landscape or a masterful painting, and there's no sexual desire connected to it.

I definitely experience aesthetic attraction. There are certain people or certain types that will draw my eye, but I have no desire to have sex with them, I don't picture them naked, I don't really even want to talk to them. I just like the way they look and they stand out to me for some reason.

Are asexuals only romantically attracted to other asexuals?

No, not necessarily. Love is blind and doesn't really care about the other person's sexual orientation. Very often asexual people will end up in relationships with non-asexual people.

And how does that work out?

It works out like any other relationship. Most of them fade away within a few months, some will last a year or two, sometimes they'll move in together, maybe even get married, have children, get divorced and end up in a bitter custody dispute. You know, the usual.

No, I mean, how does a rela- Wait... Have kids? What?

Asexual people aren't inherently incapable of having sex, and they're not inherently infertile. Since asexuals generally can have sex and are generally fertile, I'll let you figure out the rest.

Okay, that brings me to the point. How does a relationship work between someone who wants sex and someone who just isn't interested?

Sometimes it just works. If the non-asexual partner has a low sex drive or the asexual partner is willing to have sex as often as the other partner wants, then it may be a non-issue.

Sometimes it's difficult. If the asexual partner doesn't want to have sex or isn't willing to have sex as often as the non-asexual partner would like, then there could be trouble in the relationship. Often both partners will have to compromise in some way, but if both partners are committed and loving, they may find a way to make it work.

Sometimes it doesn't work at all. If the asexual partner flat out refuses any kind of sexual activity and the non-asexual partner requires it three times a day, and neither party is willing to give, that relationship will not last. It will probably end in a pit of misery and resentment on both sides.

Sometimes it's comically misguided. Like when the asexual partner talks about the sexual activities of night before with all the passion and fire of an economics textbook. Not that I know anything about that...

Under the Ace Umbrella: Demisexuality and Gray-asexuality

I've heard about something called the "Ace Umbrella". What's that about?

There's a gray area between asexuality and non-asexuality. Some people say that they occasionally experience sexual attraction, yet still relate to asexuality. The ace umbrella encompasses asexuals, as well as people in this gray area.

Some people, known as "gray-asexuals", experience sexual attraction infrequently or not very strongly or possibly aren't quite sure whether or not what they experience is sexual attraction. One subtype of gray-asexuals, known as "demisexuals", can experience sexual attraction only after developing a close emotional bond with someone.

So, if asexuals don't experience sexual attraction and these people do, why the "umbrella"? What do you have in common?

Many graces and demis tend to feel alienated by or disconnected from the sex-charged culture that they see around them. Most of the time, they do not experience sexual attraction, same as asexual people. When they do, the manner or frequency with which they do does not align with how "everyone else" describes their experience with sexual attraction. In this way, their experiences are often very similar to the experiences of asexuals.

Many times, demisexuals and gray-asexuals will even identify as asexual or something like "asexual with an exception". The frequency of sexual attraction may be so low that they go years without feeling it, so, for all intents and purposes, they are equivalent to asexual during that period.

But isn't that just "Normal" sexuality? Most people aren't attracted to everyone all the time.

Certainly, most people don't feel constant sexual attraction. However, most people seem to feel it fairly frequently. Often it's toward a romantic partner, but throughout the day, there might also be the hot co-worker or the random stranger on the sidewalk or the celebrity with the great body. Even if most people don't act on it, the attraction is still present. Grays and demis aren't like that. For a gray-asexual or a demisexual, there may be years between episodes of sexual attraction or there may have been only one person that's ever caught their eye.

So… "Demisexual"? Does that mean they only sleep with demi-gods? Demi Moore?

Unlike "hetero-" or "homo-" or "a-", etc., which describe the gender(s) that a person is or isn't attracted to, "demi-" describes the circumstances in which a person may experience sexual attraction. Demisexuals are only capable of feeling sexual attraction after they've developed a close emotional bond with someone. Even then, they still might not feel anything.

It sounds like demisexuals are trying to make themselves out to be special because they only have sex with people they love.

Demisexuality is about attraction, not action. It doesn't mean that people are picky about their sexual partners. It doesn't mean that they're "saving themselves for the right person". When someone says that they're demi, they mean that they can't experience sexual attraction unless they're close to someone. They're not choosing to repress sexual feelings for others because they don't have anything to repress.

Furthermore, demisexuality says nothing about who a demi has sex with, or if they even have sex at all. It's possible to be demisexual and a virgin. It's possible to be demisexual and repulsed. And it's possible to be demisexual and sleep with anyone who is willing. Demisexuality is only about the circumstances where one can experience sexual attraction, not about sexual activity.

It's also important to note that demisexuality is not, in any way, a value judgment against other people. Just because they only experience sexual attraction after developing an emotional bond, that does not mean that they feel there's anything wrong with people who don't require that bond to experience sexual attraction.

Okay, so they're only sexually attracted to people that they love?

Not necessarily. The close emotional bond does not have to be love. It could be friendship, it could be a work relationship, or any number of other strong emotional connections. Something purely platonic might still be capable of triggering sexual attraction.

How long does it take a demisexual to develop sexual attraction after forming the emotional bond?

Every situation is different. Many demis say that it can take anywhere from months to years to come about. Maybe less time, maybe more. It's not like there's an hourglass that's turned the moment you meet someone, and if you don't feel sexually attracted to them by the time the sand runs out, you're not going to.

Are gray-a's just asexuals who have sex?

It's not about what someone does, it's about what they feel. If an asexual has sex, they're an asexual who has sex, not a gray-asexual. If an asexual masturbates, they're an asexual who masturbates, not a gray-asexual. The difference between "asexual" and "gray-asexual" is one of attraction, not behavior.

It's not about enjoying sex, either. If an asexual likes sex, they're an asexual who likes sex, not a gray-asexual. It's possible to enjoy sex and sexual activities and not experience sexual attraction.

How can someone be "Gray"? You're either asexual or you're not. Clear as that.

Is it clear where you fit if you've only felt sexual attraction once in your entire life, then never again? Is it clear where you fit if you occasionally feel something that could potentially be sexual attraction, but it's so weak that a passing breeze is enough to make it stop? Is it clear where you fit if you're sometimes sexually attracted to people and you like sex, but don't feel any drive to seek it out and would be fine without it? Is it clear where you fit if you're not sure what sexual attraction even is, let alone whether or not you've felt it? Gray-asexuals live in this land of confusion.

So what is gray-asexuality, then? The description you're giving is a bit fuzzy.

The definition of "gray-asexual" is intentionally vague. It's meant to be a catch-all for anyone who feels they fall somewhere near asexual on the spectrum between "sexual" and "asexual". There's no strict criteria for what makes someone "gray", there's no shining dividing line. If there were, it wouldn't be a gray area.

It's a bit like the purple spectrum between red and blue. When you're close to red or blue, the color can be described as "reddish" or "bluish". There's no clear line where being "reddish" stops, but it's clear that it stops somewhere. I mean, you can't be one tick away from blue and still describe the color as "reddish". Gray-asexuality is sort of like "asexual-ish".

Do demisexuals and gray-asexuals fall in love?

Like asexuals, graces and demis come in all flavors of romantic orientation. Someone can be a heteroromantic demisexual or a panromantic gray-asexual. For a demisexual person, a romantic relationship could potentially be the catalyst for sexual attraction, however, it won't necessarily happen just because someone's in love.

Gray-asexuals and demisexuals can be even aromantic and not be romantically attracted to anyone. Additionally, a person can be demiromantic or gray-romantic, which are similar to being demisexual or gray-asexual, but around romantic attraction, rather than sexual.

How can you know you're demi or gray and not asexual?

Well, if you sometimes experience sexual attraction, that's a pretty good sign that you're not asexual.

Aside from that, if you feel like you're almost asexual, but not quite for some reason, then perhaps gray-asexual would be a better fit. If you're asexual most of the time, but there's that one person you're close to who's an exception, then maybe demisexual would work.

How can you know you're asexual and not demi or gray?

If you don't feel like you're demi or gray, then you're not. There's no 100% surefire way to determine that just because you've never experienced sexual attraction before, that you won't tomorrow. You can be fairly sure that it's not going to happen if it's never happened before, but it can't be ruled out completely.

It's a bit like a scientific theory: It can never be proven entirely, it can only be disproven. After all, everyone who has experienced sexual attraction had a first time, and they probably weren't expecting it to happen, either.

Look at it this way: There are plenty of straight people in the world. Most of them have never been attracted to a member of the same sex. But how can they know for sure that they won't be? How can they be certain they don't have dormant bisexual tendencies? The common response is "Well, I just know", but really, it's impossible to know for sure. It's not something that stresses out a lot of straight people, yet I see a lot of aces worried that they might really be gray or demi.

For me, I'm asexual. I don't expect that it'll turn out that I'm actually gray or demi, but if it does, I'm not going to push it away. If I happen to experience sexual attraction one day, then okay, I've learned that I'm not asexual after all. I'm not going to let this word that describes me very well right now tell me what to do in the future. You're not permanently locked into asexuality for the rest of your life once you've used the word to describe yourself, so if it no longer fits, don't try to make it fit.

Celibacy, Abstinence, Asexuality

I have a friend that hasn't had sex in a while. Does that mean they're asexual?

No. Not having sex makes that person celibate. It doesn't make them asexual.

But isn't "Asexuality" just a fancy-sounding word for "Celibacy"?

No, not at all. Celibacy and asexuality are two different concepts. Celibacy means someone doesn't have sex. Asexuality means someone doesn't have sexual attraction.

I still don't see how those are any different. They both mean that person isn't getting any.

Not necessarily. Asexuality describes an orientation, not behavior. Heterosexuals are attracted to the opposite sex, homosexuals are attracted to the same sex, and asexuals aren't attracted to any sex. However, it's possible for someone to have sex with someone they're not sexually attracted to. Someone can be asexual and still have sex. It's not like we're going to kick them out of the club or anything.

So... What is the difference, then?

Here's a handy-dandy cheat sheet for you:

Celibacy: Not having sex for some reason. (*"I don't have sex because _____."*)
Abstinence: Choosing not to have sex for some reason. (*"I don't have sex because I choose not to."*)
Asexuality: Not having sexual attraction. May or may not have sex. (*"Sex? What's that? Please pass the cake."*)

A lot of people try to explain the difference between asexuality and celibacy by saying something like "Celibacy is a choice. Asexuality is not." I don't agree with that characterization.

First of all, it implies that celibacy and asexuality are nearly equivalent concepts, where one is voluntary and the other is involuntary. This is not correct. Asexuality describes an orientation, not a behavior, while celibacy is only talking about behavior. Someone who is celibate is not having sex by definition, while someone who is asexual may or may not be having sex. It is possible for a person to have sex multiple times a day, yet still be asexual.

Secondly, the claim that celibacy is a choice is not always correct. A celibate person is a person who is not having sex, but the reason for them not having sex could be beyond their control. For example, someone could be in a situation where there are no partners available, or they're away from their partner for a long time, such as being locked up in prison or on the International Space Station for a few months. In that case, it's not a choice to be celibate, it's a product of their environment. Likewise, someone could be celibate because they simply don't have a partner at the moment for whatever reason. Those people may want sex and would have sex if it were available, but circumstances have forced them to be celibate. (In some cases, people have taken the phrase "involuntarily celibate" or "incel" to describe their condition. To claim that celibacy is a choice is to erase those people.) Abstinence is the choice not to have sex.

Now I'm confused. Does that mean that an asexual cannot be celibate or abstinent?

No. Asexuality and celibacy are separate concepts, however, they may overlap in an individual. Many asexuals are celibate and some are also abstinent. Filling in the blank from the definition of celibacy above, a celibate asexual is likely to say "I don't have sex because *I'm asexual and do not experience sexual attraction, therefore sex isn't all that interesting for me*." An asexual person may or may not be celibate. An asexual person may or may not be abstinent. A person who is abstinent is also celibate by definition, but a person who is celibate may not be abstinent, because they may not have made a deliberate choice to not have sex. Someone who is celibate or abstinent is not necessarily asexual, in fact, most people who are celibate or abstinent are not asexual.

It is important to note that while a person may have religious or social reasons for being abstinent, a person does not have religious or social reasons for being asexual. It can be considered offensive to assume that an asexual is "planning to wait until marriage" or wishes to "remain pure". Asexuality is not a choice, so there is no motive there. An asexual is asexual because they're asexual, not because they want to be and not because they're striving for a higher purpose. Of course, it is possible for an asexual to be practicing abstinence because of a religious or social reason, but it is the abstinence that is for the religious or social reason, not the asexuality.

In my case, I am a celibate asexual. I have not had sex in nearly nine years. I do not consider myself to be practicing abstinence because I have not made a deliberate choice to not have sex. I also do not identify as involuntarily celibate, because I'm perfectly fine not having sex. I just don't have sex because I don't have a partner and I'm not terribly interested in finding a partner. If I were to end up in a relationship with someone and they wanted to have sex, then I imagine that I would be willing to do so. (After all, that happened before.)

All asexuals are virgins, right?

No, we're not all virgins. Some of us are virgins. Some of us have had sex a few times (I'm in this group). And some of us have had a regular sexual relationship with a partner (or multiple partners).

How can you be asexual and have had sex?

Asexuality is a sexual orientation, just like heterosexuality or homosexuality. Sexual orientations are not defined by who you've had sex with throughout your lifetime, they're defined by who you're sexually attracted to. Think of it this way: A heterosexual male is heterosexual because he's sexually attracted to women, even if he's still a virgin and hasn't had sex with any women. And if there's that one night in college where he was young and confused and really really drunk and he went a little bit too far with that guy from the party because it seemed like a good idea at the time, that doesn't make him gay or bi, because his sexual orientation is defined by his attraction, not his youthful indiscretions.

An asexual who has had sex simply isn't sexually attracted to the person they've had sex with.

But, um, how can you be asexual and have had sex? I mean, physically?

Physically, there is no inherent difference between an asexual person and someone who is not asexual. We've got the same parts and pieces in the same arrangement and angles as everyone else, and they'll work the same way, too. The only difference is emotional: Who we feel an urge to use those parts and pieces with. A heterosexual person wants to use them with someone with different parts and pieces, a homosexual wants to use them with someone with matching parts and pieces, a bisexual or pansexual doesn't really care, and an asexual doesn't really feel an urge to use them with anyone else.

Asexual males can get erect and ejaculate, and the sperm is normal human male sperm, it's not some sort of magic sperm that can grow into a clone of the father on its own under the right conditions.

Asexual females can get wet and engorged and can get pregnant, and a pregnancy requires a male contribution, they're not capable of parthenogenesis.

Asexuals of any sex are capable of orgasm.

So, uh, asexual women having sex, that I get. "Lie back and think of England" and all that. They don't have to do anything. But asexual men... How does that work?

Blood fills the spongy tissue of the penis, causing an erection, and the erect penis is-

I know how it works, but how does that happen?

You mean, how can an asexual man get an erection without being sexually attracted to the person they're with?

Yeah, what's the deal with that?

Obviously, the ability to achieve erection and not be sexually attracted to the person the erection will be used with is not an isolated feature unique to asexuals. There are plenty of examples of gay men who have fathered children through natural insemination. There are also plenty of examples of men (gay, straight, or otherwise) who've left the bar at last call with whoever was willing to join them. A man clearly does not have to be sexually attracted to someone to be able to have sex with them.

I can only speak for myself here, as I've never run a survey of non-virgin asexual males regarding erectile capacity during intercourse, but here goes. Even though I'm not sexually attracted to anyone, my body can and does respond to sexual situations. It's like downstairs says "Oh, hey, SEX! I know what that is. I'll go get ready in case you need me." It'll react that way to some sex scenes in movies, or to porn, or to knowing that you and your girlfriend had planned on having sex for about a month and now she's getting into bed with you. It may be a Pavlovian response, where I know that the situation may have the reward of sexual pleasure, so my body gets prepared. Additionally, an erection can be caused by physical stimulation, regardless of the source of that stimulation. Many men have gotten erections from tight underwear, loose underwear, driving on bumpy roads, getting a physical at the doctor, or even just waking up in the morning, and none of those things are generally targets of sexual attraction. When I had sex, there was a decent period of touching and caressing prior to starting intercourse, all of which was arousing.

Some people confuse an getting an erection with sexual attraction. It is very important to note that they are not the same thing. Certainly, an erection can be the result of sexual attraction, but there are many other ways to get one (Like the physical stimulation mentioned above), and most of those other ways will work the same way on an asexual's penis as on a non-asexual's penis. When I was in the 7th grade, I used to get an erection every day in math class. Now, I like math and all, but I don't like it *that* much. Sometimes erections just happen and there's no reason for it.

Oh, and, don't forget: Despite what President Clinton may have claimed, sex doesn't necessarily require a penis to be placed within a vagina. So it doesn't require a functional penis to be involved. It doesn't even require a penis at all. Hands, mouths, and various devices and implements that may or may not be battery-operated can all be used during sexual activity.

Why bother? I mean, if you hate sex, what's the point?

Views on sex vary widely among asexuals. Many asexuals do not hate sex. There are many reasons that an asexual person might have sex. These reasons include (but are not necessarily limited to):

To please their partner.
Because they've been told, "Try it, you'll like it".
To satisfy their libido.
Because they're bored.
To find out what it's like.
Because they want children.
To "fit in" with other people.
Because it feels good.
Because they want to.

I had sex because my girlfriend at the time wanted to have sex with me. She knew that I wasn't all that interested in sex, but we figured that it was worth a shot because maybe I'd become more interested in it if I experienced it. Of course, I did want to know what it was like, since sex is supposed to be this super-amazing, mind-blowing, life-altering thing that everyone else seems to be relentlessly chasing. Something like that's gotta be good, right? But most importantly, I did it because I wanted to do it. No amount of begging and pleading would've gotten me to do anything if I didn't want to do it (Anyone who's tried to get me to eat Thai food knows that). In the end, I wasn't terribly impressed. It was okay, I guess, but nothing to get all worked up over. It just wasn't my bag.

What do you do when you have sex?

You know all the different things non-asexuals might do that they'd consider to be sex? Yeah, asexuals might do any of those. It's not like there's some ace code of conduct that says asexual women must lie passively and asexual men must thrust in the missionary position and any deviations from these standards are punishable by no cake for a month. During sex, asexual people, regardless of gender, can be as active or as passive as they want to be, and engage in activities ranging from dull to kinky.

But can you feel anything?

We can. Nothing about asexuality prevents an asexual person from experiencing physical sexual pleasure, whether that pleasure comes from a kiss on the cheek or genital stimulation. An orgasm for an asexual is no different than an orgasm for someone who isn't. Sexual response will vary from individual to individual, just like among non-asexual people. Many asexuals who have had sex have never experienced an orgasm or may experience pain during intercourse (particularly women), however, you'll find the same issues among non-asexual people, as well.

As for me, do I feel anything? Hoo-boy howdy yeah! Um, I mean, yes, I found the act of intercourse to be quite pleasurable physically.

None of this makes any sense to me. Asexuals having sex. "Asexual" means "not sexual", so it's not possible for an asexual to do sexual things. Are you sure you're ace?

I don't like the description of asexuality as "non-sexual" or "not sexual", as I feel those terms carry the implication that an asexual person has no sexual ability or is incapable of doing anything of a sexual nature or is impotent. That's simply not the case. Asexuality alone has no bearing on physical and physiological attributes and functions. I've got a penis and a pair of testicles. I can get erections. I can masturbate, lubricate and ejaculate. I can experience the intense physical pleasure of an orgasm. I can father a child. All the parts down below are present and functional, just like in any other healthy factory-original male. The only difference is that I don't have any burning interest in using those parts with anyone else, because I'm asexual. Not having any interest doesn't mean that I'm incapable of doing so.

What was sex like, from your point of view?

Somewhat analytical and disconnected. I was far more into trying to figure out what actions I was supposed to be taking at the various points in the process. *Am I supposed to kiss the breast or caress it now? Is the clitoral stimulation too fast or too slow?* I distinctly remember being bored at one point, wishing that my orgasm would arrive so that I could stop. It wasn't the epitome of all life experiences, as I'd been led to believe. But at the same time, it felt good, both physically and emotionally. The whole process felt different and in some ways better than masturbation, the warmth and the varying pressure being notable examples. And I very much enjoyed sharing the experience with the woman that I loved at the time.

Interestingly enough, I have a record of some emails I sent to my partner on the subject in the days following our get togethers. They're a monument to aceness. Instead of things like "Oh baby, you were so hot last night" and "I just got hard again thinking about what we did", these mails are full of more practical issues, like the application of lubricant, discussion of technique, and talking about how I wasn't expecting to be thirsty after sex. Anyway, here's some quotes from those mails:

"Anyway, yes, I did enjoy it. It was different than I had imagined. It took a lot longer than I was expecting (Must've gotten caught up in the rhythm and forgot to orgasm...). And it felt different, too. The way people always talk, I was expecting more of an electric explosion type of 'WowWowWOWOW!' sort of feeling the entire time. Sure, it was nice, but I don't see why it gets people acting stupid and ruining their lives and such."

"At the beginning, it wasn't that much different from masturbation and was fairly dull and repetitive, almost 'Is that all there is?' "

"Touching there, kissing here, rubbing there... It doesn't make much difference. It all feels pretty much the same to me. Stroking your breast does about as much for me as stroking your shoulder."

"Anyway, I will be willing to do it again sometime. It meets with my approval."

Your honor, I would like to submit these letters as Exhibit A for the proof of the existence of asexuality...

Um... Yeah. Wow. So, uh... What should I know if I, as a non-asexual person, want to have sex with an asexual?

As I wrote above, asexual people can have sex and still be asexual. There's nothing physically preventing most of us from doing so. However, just because someone can physically have sex doesn't mean they will want to. Many aces do not want to have sex. They may be repulsed, they may not be with the right person, it might not be the right time for them, or they may simply not want to. Even those who are willing to have sex are generally less into it and won't do it as frequently as a non-asexual partner might prefer. Trying to coerce or pressure or guilt an asexual into having sex with you is an officially uncool thing to do. "No" means NO.

Sometimes aces will be willing to work out a compromise situation when they're in a relationship with a non-asexual person, but it's important that such a compromise come from a place of respect and that the compromise be honored by both parties. The single most important thing to remember when dealing with a sexual relationship with an asexual person is that you need to talk to them. Communication. Tell them your wants and needs and listen to their wants and needs. And talk. Don't accuse and don't demand. Also, not all asexual people will be willing to compromise.

Understand that an asexual person probably sees sex in a very different way than you do. You might see it as the supreme expression of love, joining of two souls into a single blissful passion. They may see it as the rubbing of genitals against each other for a half hour or so. They may not find you sexually attractive, but that's not a personal rejection of you and there's nothing you can do about it. It doesn't mean they think you're fat or ugly or horrible to be around or they don't love you anymore. Their minds just don't work that way. You will need to learn to accept that.

One thing I've seen happen again and again is that the asexual person will gradually become less and less willing to have sex. There can be many reasons for this, and it doesn't necessarily mean that they're falling out of love. They may have come to the realization that they can't overcome their repulsion. They may have started feeling guilty that you're clearly attracted to them and they can't return the favor. They may be growing less and less comfortable in sexual situations. The novelty might be wearing off. Or they may simply not be as willing to do it anymore. You will never know what the reason is if you don't talk to them about it.

And again, no means no. If someone doesn't want to have sex with you, then they don't want to have sex with you. It doesn't matter that they're asexual. It doesn't matter if they've had sex before, even if that sex was with you. No means no.

All asexual people think the same way about sex, right? Don't you all hate sex?

Not at all, actually. The opinions on sex among asexuals are just as wide and varied as the opinions of non-asexuals on sex. Some like it, some hate it, and some don't care at all. Asexuality is only the lack of sexual attraction. Beyond that, anything goes.

Well, how do you feel about sex?

I am a "sex-positive" asexual. That may sound contradictory, but it does not mean that I want to have sex. What it means is that I'm fine with sex. I don't hate sex, I'm not repulsed by it, I don't look down on other people for having it, I'm not ashamed about the fact that I even had sex, once upon a time. I recognize that sex may be important to other people and I do not have a problem with that. I find sex and sexuality strangely fascinating, and I always have. I have a sort of detached anthropological scientific interest in the subject. Although I don't really have any desire to take part in most of the activities and practices I've heard about, I still think it's good for me to know about them, and I like learning about them. If you saw my bookshelf, you would likely not believe that I'm ace. I've got sex encyclopedias, sex manuals, books on masturbation, fellatio, and cunnilingus, even a book that describes 365 different ways to have sex, so you can do it differently every night of the year (Except during a leap year, apparently). I know about things some of my non-asexual friends have never heard of.

However, wanting to learn about sex does not mean that I actually want to have sex. When it comes to having sex with a partner, I'm largely indifferent. I don't actively seek it out. I've done it before and wasn't all that impressed, but I wouldn't necessarily be against doing it again in the right situation.

Okay, so some asexuals are fine with sex. What about the rest of them?

Not every asexual is sex-positive. Many asexuals are repulsed by sex. Repulsion goes beyond simple disinterest. A repulsed person is generally disgusted by the thought of sex or of sexual things. There are many variations of repulsion among asexuals. Some think that all sex, anywhere, by anyone, is "icky". Others are only repulsed when it comes to any form of sexual situations involving their own bodies, but are fine with other people having sex. Some repulsed people may be fine with their own bodies and may masturbate, but find the thought of doing anything with someone else disgusting. In some cases, the mere mention of an anatomical word is enough to cause someone to feel sick to their stomach.

Being sex-positive and repulsed are not mutually exclusive. It's possible for someone to believe that pretty much whatever goes on between consenting adults is fine and dandy, but at the same time be repulsed about the thought of engaging in sexual activity themselves. Part of sex-positivity is a sense of "to each their own", which means respect for how much or how little sex a person chooses to have, whether it's five times a day or zero times in a lifetime. There are no "sluts" and there are no "prudes".

Repulsion, by itself, is not necessarily an indicator of asexuality. Many non-asexuals are also repulsed by the thought of sex. They'll experience sexual attraction, but once their thoughts turn toward the act of having sex, their thoughts will be blotted out by the ickiness of the fluids and the body parts and other goings on. Some people may even mistake repulsion for asexuality, thinking that because they find sex disgusting, that must mean that they do not find anyone sexually attractive, which is not the case.

Some people have reported some measure of success in overcoming repulsion by engaging in exposure therapy. Exposure therapy is the process in which a person attempts to overcome a fear by gradual and repeated exposure to the thing that causes the fear. For instance, someone who is arachnophobic would be shown pictures of spiders in an attempt to desensitize the person to spiders. For someone who is sexually repulsed, they might try looking at pornographic images or videos, reading about sexual acts, or examining their own bodies as a way to minimize their repulsion. (Of course, your mileage may vary. I'm not a psychologist or therapist and I've never been sexually repulsed, so I might just be completely off base here. I would strongly suggest that you find someone who actually knows what they're talking about before attempting any therapy of this sort. Don't just listen to me. Also, don't blame me if you end up scarred for life after you see some of the things out there on the Internet...) It's also important to note that exposure therapy should only be attempted by those who actually want to change how they feel about sex. If you're repulsed by sex and don't really have a problem with it, then don't worry about trying to "fix" yourself, because you're not broken.

Why do I always hear about asexuals that hate sex and everyone who has sex?

I believe you're confusing asexuality with antisexuality. They are not the same thing. Antisexuals believe that sex is bad or wrong, either because of a religious objection, or because they believe that sex is at the root of many of the world's problems. While it is possible for someone to be both asexual and antisexual, one does not have to be asexual to be antisexual, and not all asexuals are antisexual. In fact, the majority of them are not.

So, do all asexuals fit perfectly into one of these groups you've mentioned?

It's possible to be some mixture of the categories I've described above, and it's also possible for someone to fall into a category I haven't mentioned. However, just because someone is asexual, you can't know which, if any, of these categories that person will be. You'll need to talk to them to find out. It's generally considered rude to assume that they're a certain way. Furthermore, it should be noted that someone's general impression of sex may not apply to every specific situation. For instance, just because an asexual is sex-positive, that doesn't mean they'll be willing to have sex with you. Communication is the key to understanding the individual.

"But asexuals can't masturbate!"

Do asexuals masturbate?
    Maybe.

"Maybe" isn't an answer.
    But it's accurate.

No, really, do they?
    No. And yes. It depends on the person.

So some asexuals masturbate?
    Correct. And some don't. It's perfectly fine either way.

Do you masturbate?
    That is an extremely personal question and is quite rude to ask. Just because I'm asexual doesn't mean that it's somehow okay to ask me that.

But do you?
    Yes. And I'm good at it, too. But if I weren't writing a chapter about asexuality and masturbation, that little tidbit would be absolutely none of your damn business.

How can an asexual masturbate?
    For the most part, they just kinda rub until-

No, I meant, how can someone who masturbates be considered asexual?
    Simple. Masturbation has nothing to do with sexual orientation. A gay person doesn't engage in some sort of homosexual masturbation. A straight person is still straight even

if they don't touch themselves now and then. It's no different for asexuality.

But masturbating is a sexual act. You can't perform sexual acts and still be asexual.

Certainly, masturbation is a sexual activity performed using sexual organs and it produces a sexual response. There's a misconception that an asexual must be devoid of all sexual properties and sexual responses and cannot experience sexual pleasure. I used to believe that myself, in fact, before I discovered what asexuality really is. I used to think that I couldn't be asexual because I masturbate. But not the case at all. Asexuality is all about attraction, not action, it's an orientation, not behavior. Being asexual does not mean one cannot or does not take part in sexual activities. Being asexual means one does not experience sexual attraction. Asexual people generally can and sometimes do take part in sexual activity. Masturbation is the most common.

Why would an asexual person bother to masturbate?

Sometimes they do it to relax.

Sometimes they do it as a stress reliever.

Sometimes they do it because they're bored.

For women, it can help with period pain.

For men, it can help with embarrassing issues like spontaneous erections or nocturnal emissions.

Sometimes they consider it a bodily function.

Sometimes they do it because their libido wants them to.

Sometimes they do it to prevent prostate cancer.

Sometimes they do it because it's like "scratching an itch".

Sometimes they like to perform a self-test to make sure everything is in working order.

Sometimes they just want to.

And, oh yeah, going out on a limb here, but could be because orgasms tend to feel good.

In other words, asexuals masturbate for pretty much the same reasons non-asexuals do.

So, it's okay to be asexual and masturbate. It's okay to like it, too. It doesn't cancel out your asexuality, it doesn't minimize your asexuality, it doesn't mean you're faking your asexuality.

How can someone who has an orgasm still claim to be asexual?

Having an orgasm does not, in any way, invalidate someone's asexuality. An orgasm is a physical response to stimulation. It's not related to one's sexual orientation, it doesn't require sexual attraction to work. To say that someone who has an orgasm can't be asexual anymore is ridiculous. When a heterosexual has an orgasm, it's not somehow a function of a heterosexual orientation. When a bisexual has an orgasm, it's not a "bisexual orgasm". So why would it be any different for an asexual? Why would the asexual orientation somehow get canceled out by an orgasm? Am I suddenly turned straight or turned gay by an orgasm? How would that happen? I wasn't attracted to anyone before the orgasm and I'm still not afterward, so if I'm not asexual anymore, what am I?

Do asexuals enjoy orgasms?

In general, yes. I know I do.

How do asexuals masturbate?

Exactly the same way someone who isn't asexual does, with all the variants that implies. There's no such thing as "asexual" masturbation. We'll use the same methods, techniques, and implements as everyone else. We'll range in frequency from absolutely never to several times a day.

"Implements"? You mean sex toys?

Yes. Like many non-asexual people, some asexuals will use sex toys to help them get off. In fact, I probably have a larger collection of toys than most non-asexual people.

(And for the record, males can and do use sex toys, too.)

But some of these "implements" are anatomically correct. Doesn't using them mean the person is attracted to the anatomical part it's a facsimile of?

Absolutely not. Anatomically correct toys are designed that way because that shape is obviously quite effective at achieving the desired stimulation. Using something that works doesn't somehow make someone less asexual. Or maybe they're using one because they liked the color or because it was in the $5 bin. It doesn't matter. Using sex toys of any kind, from a formless bullet vibrator up to a fully anatomically correct RealDoll does not mean someone is not asexual.

So, if you're not attracted to people, what do you think about while you're going at it?

Well, this is certainly different for different people, but here's some things I think about: Furniture. Vacation plans. The weather. The day at work. Things I did with my ex-girlfriend. Politics. Things I did with myself in the past. Some TV show or movie I watched. Video game music from the 80s. However, for the most part, my thoughts are "That feels good" and "That feels even better".

Wait... "Things I did with my ex-girlfriend"? How can you think about that and consider yourself asexual?

I can think about that because it felt good. I never found her sexually attractive. However, just because I never found her sexually attractive doesn't mean that I didn't find her sexually effective. When I was stimulated by her, it was extremely pleasurable and it did lead to orgasm. The memory of that sensation is extremely arousing. It's not a memory of her body or a longing to have sex with her again. I was sort of bored when I had sex with her, even though it did feel good.

Don't you ever fantasize?

Personally, I never really fantasize. I've tried, but it never works. My mind always focuses on the details and the stage direction and never on the imagining having sex part. Fantasies always seem to end up more distracting than anything. It's so much effort to get the imaginary naked woman in the right pose and performing the right motions that the slightest stray thought would kick me out of the fantasy and force me to start over. (Not to mention that the thought of the imaginary naked woman in any pose never really did anything for me...) The one that's come the closest to working is imagining myself demonstrating how I masturbate to someone else, which isn't really much of a fantasy and usually just leads to me dropping the other person and going back to just thinking "That feels good".

Some other asexuals will fantasize while masturbating. Often, they'll describe it as imagining a sexual situation with a placeholder partner. Essentially a faceless, sometimes genderless prop that's only there to provide an element that would be missing otherwise. For instance, they may imagine a person with a mouth performing oral sex on them. In this case, their thoughts are focused on the act itself and not any kind of attraction to the person performing the act. Sometimes the placeholder will be there to fulfill a fetish that the person finds arousing, in which case the focus is on the object of the fetish, and not the placeholder.

It always seems strange to me that so many people would say that you can't masturbate without thinking of someone while doing it. There's the religious thought that the reason masturbation is considered sinful is that it requires lust in the form of a fantasy, and I never understood that because I never needed lust, so why did anyone else? I would just grab it and go, without thinking about anyone. It was very mechanical. Fun, but mechanical.

How can you get aroused if you're not thinking of someone sexually?

You don't have to think of someone sexually in order to get aroused. You don't have to be sexually attracted to anyone or anything in order to masturbate. You don't have to be sexually attracted to someone to experience and enjoy an orgasm. All you have to do is touch your sensitive bits in the right way and presto! (And sometimes it doesn't even take that much...) There's a reward there that doesn't require sexual attraction. I understand that, for most people, fantasy and attraction certainly helps the process, and I'm not disputing that. But it's not a requirement.

Why would an asexual start to masturbate in the first place if they're not turned on by someone?

Any number of reasons. Sometimes they're told that it feels good and want to try it out. Other times their libido will kick in and downstairs will start screaming out for attention. And sometimes it's because they think that's what they're supposed to do, after all, it seems like everyone else is.

In my case, in fifth grade sex ed (Which was basically nothing more than a vocabulary lesson) introduced me to the terms "masturbation" and "orgasm". Masturbation was defined as "the self-stimulation of the genitals to orgasm" and orgasm was "an intense pleasurable sensation in the genitals", and I eventually put the two definitions together and realized that it was something I wanted to try. I eventually managed to work out how it was done some time later.

You mentioned a libido? An asexual person can't have a libido.

Actually, many asexuals do have a libido or a "sex drive". They'll have "urges" and desire sexual stimulation. But while for a non-asexual person, those urges tend to be directed toward another person, for an asexual, they're often directionless.

What about porn?

What about it?

Do asexuals use porn?

You're just asking that so you can say "Ha, gotcha!" when I answer, aren't you?

No, not at all. Do they?

Sometimes, yes.

Ha! Gotcha! You can't be asexual if you use porn!

I knew it...

Anyway, yes, asexuals sometimes will use porn while they masturbate. And no, it does not mean that they're not asexual.

People who watch porn don't necessarily find the performers sexually attractive. People who watch porn don't always want to participate with the performers.

Consider it another way. Watching a cooking show on TV doesn't necessarily make you want to cook whatever they're fixing on the show, does it? You might not even like whatever it is. But it's food, people are eating, and that makes you hungry. So you go get a bag of chips.

With porn, you might not want to do what they're doing, you might not even like what they're doing, but you may find it to be arousing simply because they're aroused. You watch it and think "They seem to be enjoying what they're doing. I have one of those, too, and I bet that feels good. Now I want to feel good."

Enjoying porn has no bearing on your sexual orientation. Research has shown that women who are straight will often have a strong arousal response to lesbian scenes. And the very existence of the "money shot" in porn aimed at straight men should put any argument to rest. After all, if straight men didn't find the shot of another man having an orgasm and ejaculating (Often by his own hand) to be arousing on some level, then why would it be so prevalent? It doesn't mean that the viewer is secretly gay and repressed. It just means that they don't necessarily have to feel sexual attraction toward something to be aroused by it.

In my case, I find most porn to be dull, uninteresting, and repetitive. I get more out of the sense that the performers are legitimately having a good time and experiencing pleasure than I do from the way they look or what they're doing. I am very easily distracted by things in the background, like movies on a shelf or views out the window. And things like poor lighting and poor camera work will absolutely kill a scene. Sometimes I'll watch porn for educational purposes, to see how other people do things and pick up a few tricks and techniques.

What about asexuals who don't masturbate or don't enjoy it?

Then they don't masturbate or don't enjoy it. Not every asexual has to masturbate. Not every asexual that does masturbate has to enjoy it. If you don't masturbate, there's absolutely nothing wrong with that. If it's not your thing, don't worry about it and don't worry about what other people might think. It's no one's business but your own.

Will masturbating make someone not asexual somehow?

Masturbation isn't suddenly going to make you not asexual anymore, so don't feel like you have to try it to know for sure that you're ace. I'm pretty solid evidence that no amount of masturbation is likely to change your orientation. At most, you might discover that you like the way it feels and want to keep doing it.

What about asexuals who are curious about trying it?

If you're looking for a step-by-step instruction guide, nope, not going there. I do have some other advice, though.

First: Relax.

Second: Don't turn it into a chore. Presumably you're doing it because you want it to be fun. It won't be fun if it's a chore.

Don't feel defeated if you don't get anywhere your first attempt, because you probably won't. No one does. You're not a failure and your equipment probably isn't defective. It's a learned skill and takes practice. I probably had to try for months before I got anywhere. Of course, those were the days before search engines, so it was all trial and error for me. At any rate, persistence is the key. You need to find out what works for you and not be afraid to try something new. And don't be afraid of calling in a little bit of artificial assistance. Many people, male, female, or otherwise, will use lubricants or toys to help them get off.

Don't feel guilty, as if you're betraying your asexuality. You're not.

You don't necessarily need a libido in order to become aroused. It probably helps, but it's not required. With the right mindset and the right stimulation, you can usually wake things up downstairs. Honestly, I'm not even sure I have a libido. I rarely, if ever, feel "urges" or feel "horny", or any of the other things people describe as a libido at work. Whenever I masturbate, I usually have to spend a bit of time getting myself ready. However, I have read things which claim that sexual activity itself in some cases may increase libido in a sort of feedback effect. The more you do, the more you want. So you may have a dormant libido that masturbation could potentially awaken.

And most of all, if you don't like it, stop. You don't have to do it if you don't want to. If you're not getting anything out of it, don't do it and don't worry about it.

Anything more?

I'll just leave you with this:

If you're asexual and you masturbate:
> *Then you're still asexual.*

If you're asexual and you don't masturbate:
> *Then you're still asexual.*

If you're asexual and you masturbate to porn:
> *Then you're still asexual.*

If you're asexual and you don't masturbate to porn:
> *Then you're still asexual.*

If you're asexual and you masturbate using sex toys:
> *Then you're still asexual.*

If you're asexual and you don't masturbate using sex toys:
> *Then you're still asexual.*

If you're asexual and you masturbate and you like it:
> *Then you're still asexual.*

If you're asexual and you masturbate and you don't like it:
> *Then you're still asexual.*

If you're asexual and you want to masturbate, but haven't:
> *Then you're still asexual.*

The following sections represent my personal views and my own experiences with asexuality. They do not necessarily represent the views of all asexual people. I have included them in order to provide a more personal perspective on asexuality.

What Asexuality Is To Me

I never really got sex. It always seemed alien to me. When everyone else was busy turning into horny teenagers, I was oblivious. Whatever subsystem got switched on for their 13th birthday never got enabled in me.

Whenever I looked at "sexy" celebrities, I couldn't see the appeal.

Whenever I looked at some girl I was told was "hot", I wasn't driven wild.

I never pictured people naked. I never wanted to jump someone's bones. I never felt like an uncontrollable raging horny beast.

And I never understood anyone else who did.

I've known for years that I'm not like other people when it comes to sex, but I always just thought I was simply not very good at being straight. I tried the girlfriend and sex thing, but still never felt an urge to have sex. It always seemed like everyone else was pretending and I just wasn't in on the game.

But that wasn't it. That couldn't be it. The rest of the world simply couldn't be acting all the time in such a consistent manner. If everyone was just faking it, surely someone would have pointed out that the Emperor wasn't wearing anything.

When I was 31, it finally became absolutely clear that there was something fundamentally different about me. Not necessarily wrong, not necessarily broken, just different. I was 31 years old, I hadn't had sex in over eight years, and it didn't bother me one bit.

So, if I was different, what was I? I embarked on a journey of discovery and very quickly came across asexuality, and instantly knew that's where I belonged. Everything seemed to fit and everything in my life retroactively started to make sense when viewed with this new information.

How would I explain what asexuality is like to someone who's not asexual? Well, even people who do experience sexual attraction aren't sexually attracted to *everyone.* They know what it's like to not be sexually attracted to someone. Asexuality means it's like that for me all the time, no matter who I look at.

Or for those who may be more visual: Imagine a sunset. The beautiful dance of colors, the way countless hues mix together and constantly change as the light fades. Now picture that same sunset in black and white. You can't see it. The sunset is effectively gone. Asexuality is like seeing a sunset in black and white. I know that other people can see the colors and they talk about how amazing and beautiful it looks and how their life wouldn't be complete without seeing a sunset now and then, but I just can't see the sunset. It's not there for me. It looks the same as any other time of day. But I don't feel like I'm missing out, because I've never seen it to know what it is that I'm missing out on.

Option D: None of the Above

[The following section was how I came out. I posted this up on my personal blog and let my friends and family discover it on their own time.]

There's something I want to tell all of you, so I'll get right to it:

I'm not exactly straight.

Now, that probably doesn't really come as a huge surprise if you know me. After all, I never talk about women. Classic sign of being in the closet, right?

Except no, not gay, either.

I used to think that I was straight, but not very good at it. After all, I had a girlfriend once. Sort of. And in the rare event that I've found people pleasing to look at, they've invariably been women. I just never felt compelled to try to start a relationship with any of them, and if any of them ever tried to hit on me, I completely missed the signals. I just figured I was shy or insecure or something.

Then, a couple of months ago, it suddenly struck me with total clarity that my perception of sex was completely different from anyone else I'd ever encountered. The way other people describe sex and desire feels completely alien to me. Everyone else seems to look at sex as one of the most important things in their lives, just after air, water and food, while I generally rate it somewhere far less important than remembering to leave home with a paperclip in my pocket. Seriously. I always leave home with a paperclip in my pocket, and if I ever happen to lose it, I always get a replacement right away, while I haven't had sex in almost nine years and I don't miss it at all. When I looked at women, I didn't imagine them naked, I imagined them playing Jeopardy. I didn't think about taking them to my bed, I thought about taking them on vacation and letting them drive.

By now, you're probably confused. I know I was. Not straight, not gay, and it pretty much goes without saying, not bi. So, what's left?

Option D: None of the Above.

It wasn't shyness, it wasn't insecurity, it wasn't repressed homosexual tendencies, it wasn't guilt. I'm just not interested in sex, that's all.

It's called "asexuality". It's sort of the fourth orientation, alongside heterosexuality, homosexuality, and bisexuality. Straight people are attracted to members of the opposite sex, gays are attracted to the same sex, bi people are attracted to both, and aces aren't attracted to anyone.

That sense of stunned disbelief you're probably feeling right now ain't got nothing on what I went through when I found out myself. Gotta tell ya, it's quite the experience to watch your entire life get rewritten by a single discovery. You know those movies with the twist endings, where there's some big unexpected reveal that completely changes EVERYTHING that had happened up to that point? Yeah, my life did *that*.

Then again, if you know me, you're probably not stunned at all. You're probably thinking something along the lines of "Really? That's it? You're just now figuring this out? What took you so long? I knew that YEARS ago..." I mean, nothing changes at all. I'm still me, just like I was last week or last year. All this means is that I have a name for how I feel.

So anyway, there you have it. If you think that I'm just making it up, I'm not. It's on Wikipedia, therefore it must be true: http://en.wikipedia.org/wiki/Asexuality

To my parents: Sorry that you're finding out about all of this in this impersonal way, but come on, you already knew. I'm in my thirties, I've only had one girlfriend, and I'm clearly more interested in my video game collection than women. What did you think was going on?

To my brother (and sister-in-law): Thanks for giving our parents some grandkids so I don't have to.

To the ex-girlfriend: Sorry for wasting your time and all that. At least it wasn't just you.

To my coworkers: Be honest now... There had to have been speculation going on. Probably a betting pool, too. Did anyone win?

Q & Ace

[After my "coming out" post, I wrote up this series of questions and answers in order to further explain asexuality to my friends and family.]

So, wait, what? You're... Huh? What's going on again?

I'm asexual. It's a bit like being straight except I'm not into women.

Oh, so you're gay?

No. Asexual. I'm not into men or women.

So, you're a woman trapped in a man's body?

No, I'm not transgender. I'm quite comfortable with the factory original parts and don't see any need to replace any components.

Are you missing pieces down below?

Uh, I don't think so. Let me check...

...

Hang on a sec...

Ah, found it. Nope. All present and accounted for.

So, then, you're saying down below doesn't work or something?

Down below works just fine. It's just I have no desire to interface my down below with anyone else's down below.

You can clone yourself then?

No, different meaning of the word. Although, I'd have to say that binary fission would be an awesome trick for parties.

Does that mean you like animals or something?

No. No no no. Are you paying attention? Where did you get that from? Just no.

What are you talking about, then?

Asexuality means I don't experience sexual attraction. That's it. While other people are on an unending quest to find someone willing to test the repetitive compressive stress tolerance limits of their furniture, I'm on an unending quest to find a complete set of game cartridges for the Nintendo Virtual Boy. I'm simply not interested in having sex, although the customs and practices can be rather intriguing from a scientific or anthropological point of view.

You don't want sex?

Right.

What, is it against your religion?

No.

Were you abused, then?

No.

Repressed or repulsed or something?

No.

They have a pill for that, you know.

That's not what the pill is for. The pill is for people who are ready and willing, but not able. I'm perfectly able, just not ready and willing. Saying there's a pill that'll fix asexuality is like saying there's a pill that'll fix homosexuality. I'm not going to take a pill, feel a stirring in my loins, and suddenly want to sleep with the next woman I see.

What is wrong with you? Sex is AWESOME!

You can keep your sex. Red Alarm is awesome. It's like a full 3D version of Star Fox and-

You should try it some time. You might like it!

"You do not like them. So you say. Try them! Try them! And you may. Try them and you may, I say!"

I did try it. I didn't care much for it. I mean, it was okay, I guess, but nothing spectacular. Nothing close to what all of you claim. Kinda boring, actually.

Wait, you had sex? Gotcha! That means you're not asexual!

I had sex twice. Nine years ago. Call it a youthful indiscretion or whatever. I didn't know I was ace at the time. I thought I was straight and that sex was what I was supposed to do at some point, and she offered. It seemed like a good idea at the time.

Asexuality is a sexual orientation, just like being gay or straight. Orientation is not the same as behavior. A little bit of experimentation in college doesn't make someone gay. A lesbian who wants a child and opts for natural insemination isn't suddenly straight. I had sex for the experience and because I thought that doing it might make my libido turn on. It didn't.

I don't regret it at all. In fact, I think it's good that I did try it, otherwise I'd probably have doubts that I'm really asexual because there'd be that chance that I would like it if I just tried it.

Maybe she just wasn't any good. If you find someone good, you'll change your mind.

Maybe she wasn't. I don't know. I don't have any other data points to compare. But that's irrelevant. I wasn't put off by a bad experience. I never was really all that interested in it to begin with. She could have been the most mind-blowingly skilled woman on the planet and I still probably would have said "Meh".

It's just a phase. It'll pass.

19 years since puberty is "just a phase"? Well, I'll give it another 20 minutes, but that's it!

You could be a late bloomer.

I'm in my thirties and I've never been sexually attracted to anyone, not even a naked woman standing directly in front of me. That's not a late bloomer. Nothing was planted in my garden.

I'm so sorry for you. It must really suck for you.

No, it's absolutely fine, actually. I don't want sex. It's not like I'm yearning to get laid but can't, leading me to be a pent up bottle of frustration and sadness. I'm not missing out on anything because I've never felt anything to miss out on. It would be a bit like me telling you that your life must suck because you don't want a copy of a game like Space Squash. You'd give me a funny look and shake your head in confusion over how I could possibly think that you'd be interested in that.

But sex is awesome! Everyone wants sex!

You can't see me, but I'm giving you a funny look and shaking my head in confusion over how you could possibly think that I'd be interested in that.

By the way, weren't these supposed to be questions?

Oh, right. So, uh… Aren't you just putting a fancy name on celibacy?

No, not at all. Celibacy is the condition of not having sex, while asexuality is not feeling sexual attraction toward anyone. Think of it this way: Celibacy is "I don't have sex because _____." As in "I don't have sex because it's against my religion" or "because I can't find anyone" or "because I'm in prison". Asexuality is "Sex? Whatever. Please pass the cake." So yes, I am celibate, but I'm celibate because I'm ace, not because I made some life choice to never have sex or just haven't been able to get laid and have given up trying.

Not all celibate people are asexuals, and not all asexuals are celibate.

What you're saying is that you can't get laid and have given up trying?

Um. No. I've never even bothered trying because it's just not that interesting to me. When I did have sex, it was entirely my partner's idea, and it took a lot of persistence on her part to get me to the point where I said yes.

That's a bit like claiming that I'm not interested in golf because I'm no good at it. No, I'm not interested in golf because it's *golf* and it's not interesting.

(Unless it's Golf for the Virtual Boy. I don't have that game yet...)

Why do you hate sex?

I don't hate sex. I just don't care about it. As far as aces go, I'm fairly sex positive. I'm not repulsed by it and I don't have any problem with it. In fact, I find it secretly amusing when someone thinks that I'm offended by a sexual conversation and tries to steer things in a different direction. If I seem offended, it's probably because I'm zoning out and not paying any attention because I have nothing to add to the conversation.

In the right situation, I might even be willing to give it another go. I just don't feel any need to find myself in the right situation.

Anyway, go forth and fornicate, just keep your damn kids off my lawn.

So you can't fall in love?

I can and I have. It's definitely more than a friendship, it's just not tied to sex.

Wait, how can you fall in love and still call yourself asexual? If you fall in love, you're straight, gay, or bi. Pick one.

Sex does not equal love. Sexual attraction does not equal love. Many people are sexually attracted to people they do not love. Many people love people they are not sexually attracted to. And clearly, many people love people they do not have sex with. Asexuality is the lack of sexual attraction, not the lack of capacity for love.

You're just inexperienced. If you get out there and keep trying, you'll come around.

Did you have to "get out there and keep trying" to decide you were interested in sex in the first place? And who knows, maybe you'll really get into gay sex if you just "get out there and keep trying". After all, how can you say you're not gay if you haven't tried it out?

And that wasn't a question.

But you're like totally socially inept. Sometimes you don't even want to go outside if there are people on the street. Ever think that maybe you're not asexual, but that you really just have some sort of social anxiety disorder?

I can't imagine that my social anxiety issues would cause me not to feel attracted to anyone. It's not a matter of just being too nervous to ask someone out on a date. If that's all it were, I would still likely feel attracted, but be unable to approach them. On the contrary, I think asexuality and the social issues have a symbiotic relationship going on. I'm not attracted to anyone, so I never feel compelled to break out and try to talk to someone that I'm attracted to.

Then again, maybe both are caused by my deep-seated fear of having to share a closet with someone.

So, uh... Do you feel anything, uh, down there?

Of course I do. There's nothing physically wrong with my body.

Wait a minute, how do you know that?

A: Like I said, I've had sex.

B: Equipment is tested regularly and has been found to be functioning within normal operating parameters.

So, that means you, uh...? How can you be asexual if you...?

That has absolutely nothing to do with asexuality. Like I've said, asexuality is an orientation. It relates to who I find sexually attractive, namely, no one. You don't need to find anyone sexually attractive for that, it's a physical response.

Of course, that's absolutely none of your business, but anyway...

Have you ever thought that maybe you haven't met the right person yet?

Right, maybe I haven't. But given that I've never found anyone attractive in all the years I've been looking and that everyone else seems to find multiple people attractive EVERY DAY, I think it's fairly safe to say that she's not hiding behind a tree, just waiting for me to walk by.

Why did you choose to be asexual?

It wasn't a choice. As the song goes, "baby, I was born this way." (Of course, the song doesn't mention asexuality, but whatever. We're there in spirit.)

How did you realize you were asexual?

A few months ago, I realized that I didn't think about sex the same way as anyone else I'd ever met. I started to explore those feelings and came to discover that I wasn't really interested in sex at all. And I've always been that way. During puberty, as a teenager, when I had a girlfriend, and now as an adult. I didn't really understand it. There weren't any signs that my hormones were awry and I wasn't depressed. Perhaps most significantly, I hadn't had sex in eight and a half years and it didn't bother me at all. Everyone else seems like they'd go insane if they hadn't had sex in eight and a half days.

So, I was a mystery to myself, a puzzle to be solved.

I like solving puzzles.

And so I went looking for answers. Asexuality was the one that fit the best, so I took it.

But hey, I'm a scientist. I go with the theory that fits the evidence. Right now, the evidence points toward my being ace. But in the future, I recognize that there may be some new evidence that'll come along and disprove the theory. Should that happen, I'm willing to go where that leads.

Ace? What's that?

Ace...xual. It beats "amoeba".

Why are you telling me all this, anyway?

To spread awareness and hope it'll contribute to a better understanding of asexuality. I see other aces facing ignorance and struggling with those who are unable or unwilling to understand.

On top of that, asexuality is almost completely invisible. I mean, I've felt this way for at least 19 years, since puberty, possibly even earlier, and I didn't even know this was an option until April.

I've been a supporter of gay rights for years. It would be hypocritical for me to be open in my support there, yet be completely silent about who I am, now that I know who I am.

I know that one of the greatest factors in someone being willing to accept homosexuality is to know someone who is gay. I know that if I'm open about who I am and how I feel, that all of you will gain a greater understanding of asexuality and be more willing to accept us. You won't see asexuality as some scary alien concept. You'll see me. (Granted, *I* can be a scary alien concept at times, though...)

So why have you been hiding all this time, then? What took you so long to come out of the closet?

I haven't been hiding. I really just found out myself back in April. I've been confirming the hypothesis since then and trying to figure out how to say anything about it. And it's not like I've been trying to pass or anything. Even before I made the discovery, I never went around claiming to be sexually attracted to anyone. I'm sure all of you who know me had already figured out that there was something off here. I mean, you've all seen that picture I have on my desk in the office, right?

(I'm not really sure aces come out of the closet, though. I think we come out of the pantry, because of the cake.)

Cake?

Yes. We have cake. That's how we recruit people.

Recruit people?

Of course. Just like any other sexual minority, we recruit people to help carry out our sinister agenda.

Sinister agenda?

Yes. Say, would you like some cake?

Sex

I'm asexual.

But...

I've had sex. It wasn't a compromise. It wasn't solely for her pleasure. It wasn't to save the relationship. It wasn't a violation.
I did it for me. I did it because I wanted to experience it.
On the whole, it was positive. It felt good. I liked it.

But...

It wasn't the mind-blowing experience I was led to believe. It didn't sexually awaken me. I didn't start craving sex with every waking hour of my life. I felt like I was acting.
That was nine years ago. I haven't had sex since. I don't miss it.

But...

I'd do it again in the right circumstances.

Attraction

The words "hot" and "sexy" might as well be in a foreign language. I don't relate to them at all. They always seem to be used to describe people or things that I find artificial, impractical, and unappealing.

I had a girlfriend once who complained that I thought she was "cute". She didn't want to be "cute", she wanted to be "hot".

My brain is simply not wired to understand it. When someone says "Check her out, she's so hot", what I see is someone with oversized lips, plastic skin, breasts that'll make her lose her balance, a face with more paint and spackle on it than my house, and it's all wrapped up in clothes that cannot be comfortable to wear. Those features stand out and scream that I'm looking at an artificial creation instead of a person.

I'm not saying that it's wrong for a person to like that sort of thing. I'm just saying that I can't.

I do experience aesthetic attraction. There are certain people or types of people that I do enjoy looking at. Those people will stand out and I will notice them. But all I want to do is look. It's like I'm looking at a cute puppy or beautiful picture.

Those are words I understand. "Cute", "Beautiful", sometimes even "Pretty". I see people who I consider cute or beautiful. There is always something about them that will stand out. Maybe it's the clothes, maybe it's the hair, maybe it's the smile. But whatever it is, it always feels natural. It feels real.

But even so, I get the feeling that I experience aesthetic attraction even less often than most people experience sexual attraction. It's a rare feeling.

Porn

Yes. Porn.

I've looked at porn before. In fact, porn is a big reason how I knew that I was different sexually than most other people.

You see, everyone else seemed to really like porn. Really really like it. And I didn't. Not all of it, anyway. After I got past the initial rebellious feelings of "OOH, I'M LOOKING AT BOOBIES!", I just felt bored.

Yes, *bored*.

I was supposed to like it. I was supposed to fantasize about taking part in every scene. I was supposed to turn into a drooling horn dog at the mere hint of an exposed nipple.

But I just didn't.

It was repetitive.
It was fake.
It looked uncomfortable.
It was formulaic and predictable.

Thoughts ran through my mind...

No one ever does those things.
That would pull a muscle.
The camera angle is horrible.
The lighting is horrible.
Why is she pretending to have an orgasm when no one in scene is touching anything capable of producing that reaction?

I didn't want to do pretty much anything I saw. I could not imagine myself in the scenes.

I wasn't disgusted by it. (Well, most of it, anyway...) I didn't have a moral objection to it. But I wasn't all that excited by it, either. Yes, I would sometimes get aroused, but more often than not, I'd become distracted by poor staging or unrealistic activities and lose the arousal before I could really put it to good use. (Yes, I'd get aroused. Arousal is not the same as attraction. I'd get aroused because, well, it's sex, and some part of my brain knows that sex thoughts should produce an erection because sex thoughts may be followed by sex. Plus, being the owner of one of the sets of equipment shown in the videos, I knew that some of the activities would be pleasant, so a signal would get sent downstairs to prepare it for those sorts of pleasant activities.)

Sometimes I'd pause the videos and look in the background to see what books or movies or games they had on a shelf, or to figure out what city was in the background out the window. Little mysteries like that were often far more entertaining than the repetitive in-out-in-out mechanics in the foreground.

At first, I just thought that I hit a bad batch. Like maybe everything I looked at just wasn't all that good. There were a few pictures of "cute" girls that were nice to look at, but I didn't find any "hot" girls that I'd like to have my way with. That's what porn is supposed to be all about, right? So I went exploring. Surely there was something out there I'd like.

Maybe I'd like blondes.
Maybe I'd like brunettes.
Maybe I'd like black women.
Maybe I'd like Asians.
Maybe I'd like redheads.
Maybe I'd like skinny girls.
Maybe I'd like fat girls.
Maybe I'd like goths.
Maybe I'd like S&M.
Maybe I'd like grannies.
Maybe I'd like nannies.
Maybe I'd like shaved.

Maybe I'd like natural.
Maybe I'd like cheerleaders.
Maybe I'd like lesbians.
Maybe I'd like gay men.
Maybe I'd like two on one.
Maybe I'd like three on one.
Maybe I'd like big breasts.
Maybe I'd like flat chests.
Maybe I'd... Maybe...

Maybe not.

I went through just about every permutation, combination, variation, deviation and perversion that's on the Internet and virtually none of it appealed to me in any way.[8] The vast majority of it was dull and boring. The more it turned to stereotypical "porno movie with porn stars" (You know, the "Did you order a pizza, ma'am?" variety), the less appealing it became.

That bothered me. I was supposed to like it, right? I mean, I was supposed to have a primal reaction. There were supposed to be urges and all that. Everyone else got all excited by it and talked at length about all the hammering, nailing, screwing, and various other assorted construction-related metaphors that they fantasized about doing with this porn star or that porn star. All I got was a feeling that I'd wasted my time and money.

It wasn't until I discovered that I was asexual that I realized what was going on. It wasn't that I just hadn't found some narrow subniche that would do it for me, it wasn't that I'm just

---

[8] Well, okay, there was a bit of aesthetic attraction toward the redheads, but other than that...

picky, it's that nothing would really do it for me, ever. Porn would never trigger the emotional reaction in me that it did in other people. Where other people saw a stream of fantasies and desires, I saw a poorly filmed video of mostly naked people doing things to each other that neither one really seemed to be interested in being a part of.

Now that I know I'm ace, I've gone back to look at porn from time to time. I've realized that the stuff that I do find interesting is almost always well-lit, well-framed, in-focus, it has a pleasing array of colors and shapes, and the people in the shot generally seem to be willing and engaged. In other words, it seems to be far more important to me that the picture be a good photograph in general, rather than necessarily be erotic or revealing or whatever.

So, in conclusion, what I guess I'm really trying to say here is: If you happen to make homemade porn videos, buy a bright light and a tripod and smile once in a while. Seriously.

Love

I've been in love before.

She invaded my dreams. She monopolized my thoughts. I'd talk to her for hours every day. I'd smile whenever I saw anything that reminded me of her. I'd laugh about something she said days after she said it.

I wanted to spend every moment with her. I wanted to share my life with her. There were no secrets.

I saw her face when I closed my eyes, I felt her touch after she was gone, I smelled her hair on the breeze, I heard her voice in the silence.

She was everything to me.

I just wasn't all that interested in sleeping with her.

I was watching a TV show today when a familiar scene came on. There was a woman who was interested in a male character, and in order to make her intentions clear, she physically forces herself on him as he sits in a chair. Usually, this scene leads to one of the following outcomes:

A: Sex
B: Someone walks in on them and interrupts (And they typically end up having sex later anyway)
C: Outright refusal (And they typically end up having sex later anyway)

Today, it got me thinking: What would I do in this situation?

Then I remembered... I've actually been in this situation, so I know exactly what I'd do.

I just sat there.

It was almost ten years ago now. I was meeting an Internet friend for the first time. She had made her feelings for me quite clear, but I didn't feel the same for her. I expected some sort of physical display of affection, a hug, maybe a kiss. I knew it would probably be awkward and I almost didn't want to meet her because of it.

We'd been together for a couple of hours when she told me that she wanted to sit for a bit. We were on the fourth floor of a university building and there was a small study lounge at the end of the hall. We sat and chatted a bit while looking out the window.

Then she *pounced*.

She flew over into my seat and pressed herself against me. With one hand, she rubbed my chest, the other hand ran through my hair. She pressed her lips against my neck.

I just sat there. I watched the people in the courtyard below.

I couldn't push her away because that would kill her.
I couldn't actively take part because that would be a lie.

She pressed closer.

I felt like I wasn't there. If I were there, I'd react. I'd want to kiss her, to touch her. But I didn't feel anything.
Why didn't I feel anything?
Here was a friendly, attractive woman who obviously wanted me. No one had ever expressed an interest in me like this before. She wanted to do this for months. I wanted nothing.

And I just sat there.

This isn't right.
Why didn't I want her?
Why didn't I feel anything?
Why couldn't I feel anything?
What is wrong with me?

I watched the people in the courtyard below.

I replayed that moment in my mind over and over in the days that followed. The weeks, the months, the years that followed. I searched for clues, for hints, for anything that would help to unlock the mystery of my heart. There was nothing there to find.

When I discovered asexuality, this memory was one of the first that jumped to mind. Everything finally snapped into place and became perfectly clear to me. Nothing was wrong with me at all. That's just not the way I'm wired.

Abstinence: Not participating in sexual activity (often specifically partnered sexual activity) by choice.

Ace: Colloquial abbreviation of "asexual". Often used to refer to asexual people in a similar manner as "gay" or "straight" are used to refer to homosexual or heterosexual people.

Ace Spectrum: The grouping of asexual, demisexual, and gray-asexual under a single umbrella of related sexual orientation.

Aesthetic Attraction: Non-sexual/non-romantic attraction to the way someone looks. Often described as the desire to "admire someone like a painting", but not necessarily anything further.

Affectional Orientation: See "Romantic Orientation".

Antisexual: General dislike of sexuality or sexual activity, including instances where other people are involved. Often accompanied by the belief that sex or sexuality in any form is "bad" or "wrong". Antisexual views should not be confused with asexuality.

Aromantic: A romantic orientation characterized by a persistent lack of romantic attraction toward any gender.

Arousal: Being "turned on", generally accompanied by a physical genital response, such as erection and/or lubrication.

Asexuality: A sexual orientation characterized by a persistent lack of sexual attraction to any gender.

Biromantic: A romantic orientation characterized by romantic attraction to both males and females.

Bisexual: A sexual orientation characterized by sexual attraction to both males and females.

Black Ring: When worn on the middle finger of the right hand, a black ring is an indicator that a person is asexual.

Cake: Better than sex. Also better than pie.

Celibacy: Not participating in sexual activity (often specifically partnered sexual activity) for any reason, not necessarily because of a personal choice.

Coming Out: The act of revealing one's sexual orientation to others.

Demi: A colloquial abbreviation of "Demisexual".

Demiromantic: A demiromantic does not experience romantic attraction unless they have already formed a strong emotional bond with the person.

Demisexual: A demisexual does not experience sexual attraction unless they have already formed a strong emotional bond with the person. The bond may or may not be romantic in nature. Please note that there is a difference between demisexuality, which involves attraction, and "I don't have sex unless I love someone", which has to do with behavior.

Erasure: How can I explain when there are few words I can choose? Sometimes, when people talk, they'll hideaway other people's sexuality. I don't know why. When this happens, it tends to turn the love to anger. Stop! It doesn't have to be like that. I say, I say, I say: "I know it ain't easy to see the truth, but reach out and gimme gimme gimme a little respect, and live in harmony, harmony."

Grace: A colloquial abbreviation of "Gray-Asexual".

Gray-A: A colloquial abbreviation of "Gray-Asexual".

Gray-Asexual: A gray-asexual may infrequently experience sexual attraction or may experience low sexual desire, yet will generally identify as being close to asexual. Gray-asexuals differ from demisexuals in that demisexuals will require an emotional bond before experiencing attraction, yet graces do not necessarily require a bond. The word "gray" comes from the "gray area" between asexuality and non-asexuality.

Heteroromantic: A romantic orientation characterized by romantic attraction to the opposite gender.

Heterosexual: A sexual orientation characterized by sexual attraction to the opposite gender.

Homoromantic: A romantic orientation characterized by romantic attraction to the same gender.

Homosexual: A sexual orientation characterized by sexual attraction to the same gender.

Libido: Also called "sex drive", a libido may cause arousal and/or strong desires or urges to engage in sexual activity (although not necessarily with a partner).

Lithromantic: Someone who experiences romantic attraction, but does not desire reciprocation.

Panromantic: A romantic orientation characterized by romantic attraction to any gender.

Pansexual: A sexual orientation characterized by sexual attraction to any gender.

Pie: Better than sex. Also better than cake.

Repulsed: Feeling disgusted or put off by the thought of sex. It's not necessarily the thought that sex is "wrong", more that it's "icky".

Romantic Attraction: A sense of "I would like to be involved in a romantic relationship with that person". (Please note that "romantic" in this context does not necessarily mean flowers and sunsets on the beach and candlelit dinners.)

Romantic Orientation: A description of the gender or genders (or lack thereof) that one experiences romantic attraction towards.

Sexual Attraction: A sense of "I would like to engage in sexual activity with that person".

Sexual Orientation: A description of the gender or genders (or lack thereof) that one experiences sexual attraction towards.

Here is a list of asexuality related websites that you may find useful or interesting.

Asexuality Archive
The web page for the book you're holding.
http://www.asexualityarchive.com/

AVEN
Asexual Visibility and Education Network. AVEN is one of the largest asexual communities on the Internet.
http://www.asexuality.org/

Wikipedia: Asexuality
It doesn't exist if it's not on Wikipedia, so fortunately, asexuality has its own page.
http://en.wikipedia.org/wiki/Asexuality

Hot Pieces Of Ace
A collaborative vlog channel on YouTube on asexuality.
http://www.youtube.com/user/hotpiecesoface

#asexuality on Tumblr
Posts tagged with "asexuality" on Tumblr. (Warning: Unmoderated)
http://www.tumblr.com/tagged/asexuality

Asexuality LiveJournal Community
An asexuality themed community on LiveJournal.
http://asexuality.livejournal.com/

About the Author

About Me

I am asexual. I made the discovery in April 2011, after years of thinking that I just wasn't any good at being straight. I'm a cismale with a currently undetermined romantic orientation that lives somewhere close to aromantic, but with just enough heteroromantic touches sprinkled into it to keep things confusing. I currently live outside of Seattle and work in the software industry.

Contact Info

Web: http://www.asexualityarchive.com/
Email: ace@asexualityarchive.com
Twitter: @AceArchive

Updates

Visit http://www.asexualityarchive.com/book/ for updates.